My Single Days

1921 to 1949

BY
GEORGE BELL

EDITED BY GEORGE BELL

MY SINGLE DAYS BEGAN ON THE DAY I WAS BORN ON THE 21ST OCTOBER 1921
AND ENDED THE DAY I MARRIED RUTH M GORDON ON THE 19TH FEBRUARY 1949

www.trafford.com

North America & international
toll-free: 1 888 232 4444 (USA & Canada)
phone: 250 383 6864 ♦ fax: 812 355 4082

CONTENTS

CHAPTER 5

CHAPTER 6

APPENDICES

APPENDIX I

APPENDIX II

APPENDIX III

APPENDIX IV

APPENDIX V

APPENDIX VI

My Single Days 1921 to 1949

PREFACE

INTRODUCTION TO MY SINGLE DAYS 1921 TO 1949

This a personal story of how I saw and learned about life and conditions in Monkwearmouth, other parts of Sunderland and my adventures in other countries until the 19th February 1949 when Ruth Muckles Gordon and myself were married by Father Webber in The Church of the Good Shepherd ending my single days

From an early age perhaps from eleven I began to write notes about events that evolved around me. Some of my experiences were written into diaries and note books within days of the actual events. Unfortunately a number of those have disappeared with the passing of time.

In 1985 I entered an essay competition, the title was My First Day At Work.

My entry did not win a prize but the judges thought it`s historical content was good enough to warrant a place in Beamish Museum and asked for my permission to allow a copy of it to go there. It is there now. It was then that the idea of collecting these notes together and write an essay in longhand.

During 1994 when reading through it through I realised that what I had written was only a fraction of the events that I had experienced so I decided to add from memory the other adventures I went through. Much of this chronicle is from memory without the confirmation of my diaries etc., Nevertheless I lived and experienced them all and I am satisfied with my presentation. I copied the longhand essay account into a computer and began adding memories. There were so many of them they could not all go on one

1

disc. To record the extra memories I had to sacrifice some of the earlier text to make room resulting in three discs with a mixed chain of events. Later using a more powerful computer I loaded the text from these three discs and edited to produce this version of My Single Days 1921 to 1949. I have improved the grammar without altering the context so as to make it easier to read. I have attempted to include everything from the previous binders into this one and to write my story in a manner as near as possible to the way the events happened. To achieve this I have adopted a year by year aproach.

I was born on 21st October 1921 therefore I would be too young to fully understand what was going on during my early years. What I have written about that period will be from what I had learned from my parents, friends, newspapers and library books.

The slum clearance which started around 1930 is probably the only significant noticeable change in Monkwearmouth so I have assumed that my account of 1921- 1929 will be reasonably correct

A BACKGROUND TO MY SINGLE DAYS 1921 TO 1949

The armistice of November 1918 heralded in a new era for peace but was threatened when in 1933 Adolf Hitler (Shicklegruber on his birth certificate according to historians) became chancellor of Germany. The country was suffering from galloping inflation and he tackled the problem by giving the people work on armaments and he built up his armed forces. He then marched his troops into a couple of small states then Czechoslovakia. After each occupation that one to be the last. He then took Austria and meeting with no opposition from neighbouring countries decided to take Poland. His army invaded Poland on the first September 1939. This was his final act which plunged Europe into a lengthy war.

In 1936 the army of Mussolini the Duce of Italy invaded Abyssinia and the aeroplane pilots were blessed by the Pope before they flew over and dropped bombs and poison gas on the natives whose main weapons of defence were spears. Modern armoury was very limited.

By June 1940 the German armies had occupied Norway and overran France. The British army was saved by a miracle when forced to evacuate Dunkirk and other French ports. The airfields in Britain suffered a terrible onslaught of air raids by the lufftwaffa intent on preparing the way for a seaborne invasion of England, code name Sealion. While these raids were taking place Mussolini allied himself with Hitler. He probably thought Britain was finished.

At this time Canada, Australia, New Zealand and South Africa were so far away that Britain virtually stood alone against Germany, Italy and their satellites.

The USA probably thought we were doomed. They helped us by supplying us with raw materials but they bled us dry with very exceptional hard bargaining. They made no attempt to become too involved with us and even kept their ambassador in Berlin until the Japs raided Pearl Harbour 7th December 1941. Of course the ambassador in Berlin may have been a double agent or perhaps I have been reading too many adventure stories.

My Single Days 1921 to 1949

MY APOLOGIES FOR NAMES MISSPELLED OR OMITTED

DESCRIPTION OF MONKWEARMOUTH

This description of Monkwearmouth is how I saw it up to 1929.

After the 1914-1918 war Monkwearmouth appears to be a thriving industrial and shipbuilding district of Sunderland. It covered about four square miles with four irregular boundaries. Roughly the river made the natural south boundary and the seashore the eastern. The western border is from the Wearmouth bridge to a half a mile along Newcastle Rd, and from here eastward to the sea is the north boundary

A good place to begin describing Monkwearmouth is from the Monkwearmouth bridge which is about ninety feet above the River Wear. Below the bridge and a little to the north-west was a dry dock built into the river bank. At high tide a ship would enter or leave through the opened lock gates part of which remain today in April 2011. Nearby are the sheepfolds where cattle and sheep were auctioned every week. Just beyond were the derelict wharves where we very often played. Strictly speaking these places were in the Colliery Ward not Monkwearmouth.

On the west side along North Bridge St were the Monkwearmouth railway station, sidings and terraced houses each with a garden twenty feet long reaching to the pavement then a few wholesale butcher shops each having a very broad frontage, the main road was narrow allowing only two way traffic. In the western back lane behind these butcher shops were the slaughter houses where the animals were killed in full view of anyone passing. Common sounds to be heard day and night were the squealing of pigs and the lowing of cattle. Every day porters would carry the carcasses to lorries parked at the roadside and were then transported to retail shops around the town. From the bridge on the opposite side of the road was the Oak Tree pub now demolished, the site is now a road junction. Further along North Bridge St were shops selling fresh fish, pork and pease pudding, fresh meat, a barber, fruiterer, Smith`s funiture shop, Simmons sweets and chocolates, Cheritt the chemist, Brown the draper who was once the Mayor, Mr Truffle an Austrian immigrant who sold cigarettes and tobacco and Barclays Bank. In the backlane behind is the tramways office, tram depot and the tower clock. All of these approaches culminate in a seven roads junction and to my knowledge there is only one other to equal it in the world and it is in Paris. In the centre of this junction there was a small island where a policeman would stand controlling the traffic. The names of these streets reading clockwise are North Bridge St. back lane behind North Bridge St, Wreath Quay Rd, Southwick Rd, Newcastle Rd, Roker Avenue and Thomas St. Wreath Quay Rd has since been renamed Millennium Way.

In Roker Avenue stood the Roker Cinema, the Ryhope and Silksworth Co-op store a garage, several small shops, a Post Office and the Fort pub. On the opposite side was the replica of a lighthouse built above a shop, the Miners Hall, a shop displaying a car for £100. the Red Lion pub and the Ropery. Turn left here into Fulwell Rd passing Tyzacks brickworks and football ground. Turn east into Roker Baths Rd and follow it to the sea front passing Roker Park football ground on the way.

Go back to the north east end of the bridge and follow the river eastwards to pass Wilsons sawmill with rafts made up with many logs floating in the river undergoing a seasoning process then Palmer`s Hill engineering works, the ferryboat landing, Deucher`s brewery, Crowns and JL Thompson shipyards, then cross over Millum Terrace to Blumer`s shipyard now derelict where we sometimes played until chased by the watchman, a lifeboat slipway, an oil terminal beside the North Dock Basin and finally the

Block Yard where huge concrete blocks were made for the construction of the New North Pier. About three times a year fun fairs were staged on the Block Yard attracting thousands of people.

Many of the streets bordering these industries along the riverside were destroyed in the air-raids during 1943 and most of the surviving properties were demolished in the re-development of the area in the 1960s.

By the time I was born my Granda Blenkinsop formally a shipyard riveter had already retired from JL Thompson shipyard and opened up a second hand furniture shop in Dundas St At nights and week-ends his sons delivered furniture to customers and his daughters helped out in the shop. When I was turned twelve years old I helped by delivering small items to customers and made a bit on tips.

CHAPTER 1

1921 TO 1925

All through the 1920s there were four distinct seasons. Spring, Summer, Autumn and Winter. November was always a very foggy month some of them real pea-soupers. The winters were very cold and the first snows fell early in December and lasted close to the end of March and sometimes into April.

At the time of my birth this area was densely populated. It was common for three or more families to occupy one building and some families were quite large.

I was born on the 21st October 1921 in Murton St Nursing Home near Mowbray Park. After two weeks Mam and me were brought home to live with Dad in the downstairs front room of number 2 Dock St. East in Monkwearmouth.

The houses in Dock St. East once belonged to shipowners, ship captains and other well to do people. Some years previous to my arrival all of these people had moved to the west part of town and the empty properties were let out to tenants.

All of these houses had a front garden and a back yard. Entering through our front door into the passage with on the right a door to the front room. Opposite was a staircase leading to rooms on the next level and further up to the attic rooms. At the back of the house behind the front room were more rooms then the back yard with a wash house a cold water tap and a WC shared by all of the tenants.

On one wall in our room was a bracket supporting a gas pipe which when lit produced a naked flame giving some light and casting large dark shadows. The lighting was improved when some time later a silk mantle was placed over the jet and when lit the burning gas gave off a bright white light.

All the other rooms had their gas light suspended from the ceiling so reducing the size of the shadows

A paraffin oil lamp gave light in the passage. Mr and Mrs Hubbard and their three year old daughter Norah lived in the downstairs back rooms.

Uncle Harry, Aunt Bella my Mams sister and their three year old daughter Molly lived upstairs and had access to the attic rooms. Isabel was born on the 28th May 1921 and she shared the bedroom with her parents and Molly her elder sister.

6

1924

When cousin Harry was born in September one attic room was converted into a bedroom where for a couple of years me and my two cousins shared this room for play and sleeping. We lay head to toe, me at the bottom the girls at the top. There was no gas point in this room so at bedtime illumination was from a candle and sometimes it was from the moon. The candles and paraffin oil were bought from Tennicks corner shop.

Friday nights were bath nights and it was a strenuous time for Molly Isabel and me, all three helping Uncle Harry to carry buckets of water from the backyard cold water tap and up the stairs to be heated over the coal fire. When hot enough it was poured into a full sized tin bath. After the three of us had bathed the dirty water was emptied from the window on to the yard below.

Round about this time Mrs Hubbard gave birth to another girl, Hettie.

Our attic window overlooked Millum Terrace and I could see Blumers derelict shipyard and on the other side of the river Greenwells repair yard and Young`s shipbreaking yard. Very few sailing ships were visiting the port now. Sails were being replaced by triple expansion steam engines in ships now being built with iron plates replacing timbers. I saw two clipper sailing ships arrive in the river and berthed in Youngs to be broken up. I believe they were the last two sailing ships to come here

1925

PRE-SCHOOL

Long before I started school Uncle Jim with his younger brother Billy and friends took me to the Roker sands and to swim in the sea.

Some days I would go into the house next door to play with Jimmy Maughen and his cat while his mother was out shopping, his Dad at work and sister Lily at school.

Millum Terrace was or local playground. The pavement there was very wide with a wall over a hundred yards long. On the other side of this wall was drop of fifteen feet to the top of a clay bank. From a break in the wall was a long flight of steps in two sections leading down to the North Dock Rd. and the wet dock. The short flight stopped at a pathway where going north led to the garden allotments and the other to the North Dock Rd. and

Millum Terrace. Ten yards from the steps stood a gentleman's convenience. The second section of steps was more than three times longer than the first. A favourite pastime of ours was to slid down this clay bank. With a sheet of cardboard to sit on we started the slide from the gentleman's convenience and happily slid down the slope, walked or ran down the road to the steps to bring us back to the top and do it all over again. One day I done one slide too many. Nearing the bottom I lost control and I shot across the road and split my forehead open on the kerb.

Mr Danny Button who happened to be walking down this road at the time picked me up and brought me home.

I was then taken to the hospital in Roker Avenue where the wound in my forehead was stitched up. My troubles were not over. Later in the year I went down with double pneumonia.

I can recall being carried into a horsedrawn cab and taken to the Highfield Hospital in Hylton Rd,. Millfield which some years earlier had been the Workhouse. According to local gossip drop-outs would go there for the night and they stood on opposite sides of a clothes line, leaned against it and tried to sleep.

During the day most streets including ours were very busy. There were coal carts, taxi-cabs laundry vans, milk floats and beer drays all being hauled by horses. With so many horses on the streets one would expect them to be fouled up. That wasn`t so, within minutes of a horse leaving it`s trade mark someone would be out with a brush and shovel. It made excellent manure for the gardens and nearby allotments. Every day water carts swilled the streets and housewives step-stoned their doorsteps and kept their piece of pavement clean and tidy even during the snowy winter months.

Every day except Sunday there was a line of horses pulling carts filled with sand from the beach and returning empty to collect more.

Motor tankers were going to and from the BP petrol storage tanks on the North Dock and as they passed they shook our houses to their foundations. Motor cars rarely used our street. Most of the few that were around used Roker Avenue. Except for the Economic buses almost all traffic had ceased operating by tea-time

CHAPTER 2

1925 TO 1936

STANSFIELD ST INFANTS, BOYS AND GIRLS SCHOOL

Miss Kirton with pupils 1928

Mr Logan was the school caretaker and schoolboard man. One of his duties was to search out truants and we were more afraid of him than the teachers.

This school had the reputation of being a tough school. It was diveded into three departments, one for the girls and one for the infants both sharing a big playground.

A railing separated them from the boys who had a playground of their own. I started in the infants class after Easter and I was five years old in October. We made models of clay taken from the bank we often played on and gently eased into learning how to draw simple pictures and to write the letters of the alphabet on a slate using a special pencil..

We listened to fairy tales read from books. One of our lessons in school was about the British Empire and how great it was and how superior we were to other countries. We

˙ learned to sing God save our king, Rule Britannia, Land of hope and glory and other patriotic songs. The teachers I remember best even were Miss Kirton, Mrs Knox and Mrs Hugall. When naughty I was thumped on the back by the Head Mistress Miss Carter. On reflection her thumps would have been no more than light taps but at the time I thought I was being flayed alive. Looking back I think they were all great. For a while I was a monitor along with Stella Simpson.

Evelyn Grainger another girl in the class grew up to be the mother of Derek Robe a school friend of my second son John who are still friends in 2009Australia and Betty Dodds is the mother of Bobby Dorward a fellow member of the Clipper darts and domino club in Zetland St from 2003 to 2008. In 2009 the club members transferred to the Wheat Sheaf in Roker Avenue.

In class I sat beside Lily Richardson. After leaving school it was in Wetherall's dance hall in 1948 when we next met. A couple of weeks later she was to be married and then they were to emigrate to Australia.

1926

After school we played games in our own street and when it turned dark we moved under a street lamp. When the two Economic buses were due we stopped play and stood on the pavement until they had both passed. The games we played were mostly seasonal. Tiggy, deliver, hop-scotch, hide and seek, statues, queenie, mount-a-kitty, bowl a hoop, diablo, kittycat, leap frog, one boy carrying another on his back like horse riding, skipping singly or rope stretched across the road with several skipping together or used a rope tied to a lamp post for a swing. There was also the old recreation park at Carley Hill and a new one in Thompson Park.

Some winter nights were spent in any one of our friends houses playing boxed games such as Ludo, snakes and ladders or tiddly winks. Often parents would be around but sometimes they left us with a couple of pennies for the gas. If they forgot the light would slowly dim then go out leaving us to play in the firelight until they returned. Whether playing inside or out we all had to back in our own homes by nine-o-clock.

If not the mother of an absent child would stand outside and call for her bairn to come in, loud enough for all in the street to hear.

Electric lighting was slowly taking over from gas lamps. At dusk a lamp lighter would come to every lamp post in the area and with his pole would pull the switch and the lamp would light up. At daybreak another would go round and switch them all off.

My brother Bobby was born on the 26th July in the same nursing home as me and then came to live with us in 2 Dock St East.

Some months after starting school I was sent to Sunday School in Dock St chapel even though I had been christened in St Peter's Church of England probably because most of the bairns in our street were going there too. The Rev. I Howarth preached in the main church. Mr Pretty a teacher at Hendon Valley Rd School and his sister Mary, Mr Metcalfe the two Crinson brothers, Mr Laughterbach and his two sisters joint owners of the mineral water factory in Zetland St and Mr Wragge were all scripture teachers at Dock St Methodist Chapel. Some years later Mary was married to Mr Metcalfe. Mr Young the chapel caretaker was also the cubmaster. I joined the wolf cubs with Leslie Bearpark this year. Mr Pretty also ran a mid week youth club which I joined when I was old enough. We played games most of the time.

The Sunday School treat was a yearly event and it took place on a Wednesday afternoon during the elementary schools summer holidays. When the open charabanc arrived at the chapel we piled on board and then we were driven to a field near to the Boldon Flats which was natural habitat for frogs and newts.

We ran from the bus and carried on until we were brought to heel.

The teachers put us into age groups and organised various types of races. There was the sack. obstacle, three legged,, 50yds, 100yds, and an egg and spoon race. These were run in heats and then the winners of the heats raced again in the finals.

The winners of the finals received small prizes, none for me. Sandwiches, cakes and lemonade were handed round and to finish off sweets were scattered and we scrambled for them. On the way back we sang popular songs one of which was

"Oh the driver has got the wind up" to the tune of "John Brown's body"

1927

Where Millum Terrace joins Harbour View at Roker there are three roads.

The high road continued north to Seaside Lane. The second follows in the same direction but slopes down to the low promenade and Roker beach. The third went directly opposite and down to the Block Yard where hundreds of huge stone blocks were sculpted and used in the building of the New North Pier way back in about 1900. The completion of this pier and the existing breakwater becalmed the enclosed waters enabling a safer passage for ships sailing between the old north and south piers to or from the river. When the sea outside of the two piers was stormy it was relatively calm inside so people went there to swim rather than between the Holey Rock and the New North Pier and the area became known as the Bathing Sands and gained popularity while Hendon Beach a resort for many years went into decline.

During the summer months several Italian ice cream vendors, Fella, Geraldi, Minchella, Guidie, Louise and others parked their barrows on the road between Roker Avenue and Harbour View. When one had sold out he pushed his barrow back to his supplier and if people were still around he would return with a fresh supply of ice-cream.

It was very early one summer morning when my Dad took me to the low promenade at Roker and there joined a large crowd already waiting to observe the total eclipse of the sun. Looking across the sea I watched the sun rise above the sea. To protect my eyes I looked through a piece of brown glass from a broken beer bottle. As the sun rose the gap between the sea and the horizon widened. When it was well clear I watched the moon slowly pass across the sun blotting out the light and the sky turned dark. The seagulls which had been making a great deal of noise while flying around became quiet and disappeared. Everything returned to normal when the sun resumed command a few minutes later.. I was then taken to school.

On Sunday nights I often went with Mam and Dad to Roker Park to watch the old men playing bowls and then go to the bandstand and listen to a brass band. At the exits tarpaulins were strung out to collect pennies from the crowds as they left the park. I fished for tiddlers in the park pond or sailed my small yacht HMS Tiger. The pond was full of weeds and my boat having a long perpendicular keel was easily trapped and each time that happened I had to wait for the wind to free it. One day I was lucky. A man on his way to the beach to fish cast his line and retrieved it for me.

1928

Being overcrowded we moved to 49 North Bridge St. where Uncle Dave and Aunt Fran my Mam`s sister already occupied the upstairs flat. Mrs Weirs with her son Billy lived downstairs. Billy was at least sixteen years old, a good footballer and played for a local team. Sunderland Corporation Tramways Football Club were keen to have him so they offered him a job in the tramways if he would sign for them. He did.

We lived in the attics and my bedroom window overlooked the railway tracks and I could watch the trains go by and see the freight wagons being shunted around in the marshalling yard.

In the back yard there was a chicken house with several hens and a cockerel

and a long Run enclosed with wire mesh. The hens were laying eggs daily. Periodically a brood of chicks was hatched and brought up to a warm room until strong enough to return to the Run. My Dad looked after the poultry while Uncle Dave was at sea. Although a time served tradesman he could only get a job as a donkeyman on coaster engaged in the Home Trade. He would be away for about three weeks then have a few days at home.

Every Friday night my two cousins came up and shared the bath with me. It was great, no more fetching and carrying buckets of water.

Every Wednesday dinner time in winter I went from Stansfield St School to Aunt Bella for broth and dumplings. Also there were Uncle Harry and his nephew Kit Wharton home for dinner from JL Thompson shipyard and my three cousins.

After school and finding no children to play with in this locality I went back to Dock St East to play with my old friends. Our play was not confined to Dock St East and Millum Terrace. We were adventurous and visited the North Dock and the Block Yard at Roker, Hylton Woods and Boldon Flats for frogs and newts. The members of our gang all lived in the bottom block of Dock St East except me. They were George Holmes, Milton and Rita Jolliff, Norah and Hettie Hubbard, Stan Merritt, my cousins Molly Isabel and Harry Wharton, Jimmy Parks, Jessie Lodeman, Jimmy, Ronnie and Rosie Cutter, Leslie Rannie, George and Ethel Thompson and their cousin George Thompson, Jimmy and Lily Maughen, Teddy Mitchell, Peggy Hutchinson and myself. Jimmy Copeland lived in Lower Dundas St and we invited him to join our gang as there wasn`t one in his street. The neighbouring streets had their own gangs of boys and girls and all were known as corner enders. There were times when rival gangs would raid one another and there would be a right old skirmish. On polling days be it or local or parliamentary many a battle was fought using bashers. A basher was made up by tying a bundle of newspapers to a length of string. Street gangs would split up and the boys and girls would join rival political parties. The next day many of those who were fighting each other on the previous night would sit in class and at playtime would play together in the school yard.

Being a child I wasn't aware that the town had been slowly suffering from a depression since 1921. After the 1926 General Strike work was so difficult to find that men accepted work no matter where it was or how little the pay.

One was Mr Mushens see p102. He was Alan Aflecks uncle. On finding work in Clydeside he took his family to Scotland and settled there.

During the next few years many men finding work elsewhere moved away from the town taking their families with them.

When I was seven years old I was moved from the infants into standard 1A in the boys school. There were forty boys in this class and were still being taught by a lady teacher Miss Kirton but now learning to write in an exercise book using a lead pencil and erasing our many mistakes with an Indian rubber.

I took it as being normal to see so many men knocking around the streets. Some worked the allotments beside the clay bank above the North Dock at the bottom of my street and others kept pigeons and from what I remember most of the boys and girls in my street and school were decently dressed.

A small number appeared to have very little. Some boys came to school in their barefeet and each ear representatives of some charitable organisation came to the school and gave these boys a pair of boots. Two weeks later these same boys were barefooted again.

I was very lucky to have several uncles and aunts most of whom were not married at the time and I done well on my birthday and at Xmas for presents.

CHANGE OF HEADMASTER

When Mr Schofield our Headmaster retired at the end of the Easter term Mr Craggs from Millfield was to take over at the start of the summer term. His reputation of being a hard man who punished wrongdoers with the cat-o-nine tails came on ahead of him. At 9-00am on his first day he blew his whistle and ordered the boys to form a square. There must have been at least 500 boys aged 7years to 14

He stood in the centre and introduced himself as a man who would stand no nonsense and assumed that they the boys already knew that he had

14

no qualms about using his cat-o-tails on any boy for misbehaving himself so much that his teacher had to send him to me. I will show that boy this instrument of torture hanging on the wall and advise him not to be sent to me a second time. As far as I am aware no boy has visited his study on a second offence.

When morning school closed for dinner I often walked with a friend Bob Etherington up Roker Avenue as far as the Wheat Sheaf. Sometimes at the crossroads a group of pitmen still covered in coal dust stood chatting before going home for a bath. No pit baths or showers then.

On the day when the ice wagon was due to deliver supplies to the fishmonger in Church St I would leave Bob at the corner and go and watch the ice blocks being unloaded. These blocks were broken into small pieces and covered the fish. This helped to keep the fish fresh for a couple of days. There were very few shops with a refrigerator and even fewer in private homes so most meals were prepared and cooked on a daily basis. Butter, bread etc. was bought only in the quantities needed for the daily meals resulting in regular visits to the local shops. Dairy produce was kept in the larder on a marble slab. On other shelves were sugar, condensed milk, tea, jam and very little else.

We often had rabbit pie. The rabbit was bought for a shilling at Parkers the local fruit and vegetable shop.

Before cooking it had to be skinned and my Mam done that. On approaching Xmas for partying during the festive season stocks were built up.

One day I fell down in the school yard badly scraping one of my knees. I went alone to the Monkwearmouth Hospital in Roker Avenue for treatment and on opening the door I was met by a terrifying sight. Before me was a big room and on each of the many tables standing against the walls was a boiler which looked like a tea urn standing over a gas ring. Every boiler was belching steam filling the room with a huge cloud of vapour. I was told to sit down and the nurse looked at my knee then with one hand held it in a firm grip and with the other dipped a swab of cotton wool in the scalding water then swiftly slapped it on my knee. I clenched my teeth and gasped. Even at that early age my ego told me not to cry in front of a woman. I was a big boy. This action was repeated a few times before she finally wrapped a bandage round my Knee.

Some years later at a cinema watching the film "Dantes Inferno" where one scene was of the "Fires of Hell" brought back memories of that hospital room.

There were plans for a new hospital to be built in Newcastle Rd but a shortage of cash prevented the scheme from going ahead. I believe it was originally meant to be paid for by the Sunderland Corporation (Council).

To eliminate the shortfall sponsors were sought and our school was approached and the pupils were asked to buy little red paper bricks at a halfpenny each which when bought were pasted on to a very large sheet of white paper pinned to one wall. During the following months as the money rolled in a red brick wall was gradually built finally covering the sheet. When sufficient money had been collected the new Monkwearmouth and Southwick Hospital was built in Newcastle Rd. replacing that steam trap in Roker Avenue. With my contributions I consider myself to be a shareholder. This defunct hospital was then converted into an extension to the nearby rope making factory.

Another pastime after school or during the school holidays summer or winter was to go to the North Dock basin or the bathing sands beside the Block Yard to swim.

The sea temperature varied little between summer and winter so even with snow lying on the sands we still went swimming. On the bathing sands there were cubicles for modest bathers to change and these were wheeled to the water's edge. Sometimes I would swim in the river at Sand Point next to JL Thompson's shipyard or beside the dry dock below the Wearmouth Bridge.

1929

Mondays were always full of excitement. After school my two cousins and me dashed to Roker Avenue to see the cattle and sheep leaving Portobello Lane. Very often a bull or a sheep on their way to the Sheepfolds would run away from the drovers scattering the onlookers. When Roker Avenue was cleared of animals we raced to Grandma to be first to listen in to the Children's Hour on the BBC at 5-00pm. The BBC were transmitting programs over the air which were received by a gadget known as the Cat's Whisker and my Grandparents had one. Only one person could listen in at a time earphones had to be worn.

Drivers often parked their lorries along Millum Terrace and knowing that lorries took a long time to accelerate we sometimes played the dangerous game of hanging on to the back of one of them riding about a hundred yards before dropping off.

Another pastime not quite as dangerous was to look out for a car believed to be owned by a millionaire, registration number BR1. There were still very few motor cars around.

5 DUNDAS ST

Author with family 1936

After eighteen months living in North Bridge St my Mam understanding the present unstable work situation accepted an invitation to become the caretaker of the surgeries of Doctors James Hamilton and Dr Norah Hamilton in 5 Dundas St opposite to Grandmas shop. One of the conditions of the tenancy was that someone had to be on the premises to receive callers and to take telephone messages when the surgeries were closed. During surgery hours Miss Maughen the dispenser and the doctors were in attendance.

Dr Norah`s surgery was in the basement, Doctor James Hamilton`s surgery on the first floor and ours on the next floor up with attics above.

On this floor was the front room where my young brother Bobby and me slept in the sideboard bed. There was also a three piece suite and a piano. Sometimes I played one finger tunes on it. I didn`t have the gift my Mam had.

The small bedroom was for Mam and Dad.

On the landing was a gas cooker and a large cupboard.

The kitchen had an oven at the side of an open coal fire with a mantle shelf above on which lay ornaments and an alarm clock. In the middle was a dining table and four chairs and at the window overlooking the yard was a long table on which most of the meals were prepared. A cabinet housing a gramophone and a loud speaker, the cabinet was made by Uncles Jim and Bill and it played 33, 45 and 78rpm records There was no bathroom so to bathe I made use of a large enamelled dish normally used for washing up after meals. The hot water came from a large kettle heated over the fire. For a real hot bath I went to the Slippper Baths in High St. West.

In the back yard was a large garden surrounded on three sides by a broad concrete walkway. At one corner of the garden a big tree was growing in a rockery, an elderberry tree grew in each of the other three corners. My Dad grew vegetables an flowers, my young brother Bobby helped him but I had no interest in gardening. At the bottom was the coal-house, water-closet and wash-house with a cold water tap, coal fired copper, a bench, a poss-stick, a tub and a large old fashioned mangle. On wash days after school I turned the handle and my Mam fed the wet clothes between the rollers. Our back lane was named Back Dundas St. and on Monday mornings at seven I saw from my bedroom window a pawnshop where a long queue of people were waiting to return suits and other knicknacks they had pledged for the weekend.

Facing the front room window was the North Bridge St back lane. From Dundas St for half it`s length it was very wide. Set in this part of the road was a large weighbar on which lorries would roll to be weighed. It was controlled by a weighmaster in an office alongside who also collected the fees from the drivers. I often saw this man operating the weigh-bar but I never got to know him until many years later see p43, 54. From this point it changed into a very narrow lane with the tram shed at the east side. The local childrenn played in the big area. They were Athol and Gordon Holton, John Ward, Alan Aflick and Brian Lowe.

They were younger than me so after a while I went back to Dock St East again to play with my old crowd but still kept in touch with the Dundas St bunch and when Bobby was old enough I brought him out to play with them.

Up till this time I had only known the Blenkinsop side of my family. I never knew what the disagreement had been between the two families but one day Uncle George Bell a postman delivered some mail to us. My Mam invited him in and the rift was healed. Granda and Grandma Bell would have seen me before then but for me I knowingly met them for the first time when Mam and Dad took Bobby and me to see them at their home in 12 Reynoldson St next to the Star Public house off Durham Rd. This was a very short street and at the opposite end were some steps leading down to Robson`s flour mill in Chester Rd. Uncle George, Aunt Mary and daughter Mary lived in Potts St Millfield and I often visited them. My Dad`s sister Maggie and Uncle George Forth, sons Jimmy and George, daughter Marjorie lived in Quarry St Silksworth. I saw them most times when visiting granparents in Reynoldson St.

One day my Dad took me along North Bridge St and just before the Wearmouth bridge turned left into Bonner`s Field. At the bottom of this street my Dad pointed to a building and said that it was a munitions factory which produced Mills bombs and that he worked there as an oiler after recovering from the loss of his arm in the battle for Vimy Ridge.

A few months after moving to Dundas St Aunt Fran and Uncle Dave bought a cottage in 69 Annie St Fulwell.

When he was at home from sea I would go to see him and he taught me woodwork and I made many useful articles such as egg stands and fireside kerbs which I gave to married members within the family. There were times when he had to stay with the ship usually in Cardiff and Aunt Fran would travel down and stay with him until the ship had sailed. One time when his ship the SS Deerwood was moored at the Lambton Drops the ship`s lifeboat was brought over to the Bridge Dock to pick up my Dad and me. When we were alongside the vessel my Dad got hold of the Jacob ladder and a paddle tug-boat steamed by creating a terrific wash causing the boat to rock violently. My Dad having only one arm hung on with great difficulty. When we were all aboard I was shown into the engine room where it was explained to me how the engine, boiler and refrigerator all worked. Uncle Dave wishing to sit for his Board of Trade engineers certificate and also to safeguard his job arrangements were made for Uncle Billy to take his place for one voyage on his ship. For years the family had been visiting Grandma and Granda on a Thursday night to chat and play Newmarket a card game. Uncle Dave being successful in the examination called one Thursday night and proudly showed the certificate to all in the room. When the ship returned to England Uncle Dave reclaimed his berth. Some time later with his certificate he was able to leave the coastal trade and sail on deep sea voyages.

Uncle Bill on his return home from that voyage told us one story that when ashore in Russia he and all members of the crew were shadowed all over by plain clothes police. From there the ship called in a port in Egypt and he bought a chameleon and on his return home he gave it to me and I named it Marmaduke. It spent hours hanging on a curtain at the window catching flies, it`s tongue was hinged at the front of its mouth and it would thrust it out to snatch a luckless fly.

It lived on flies and lettuce and in the summer months we were plagued with flies and it was well fed. It had the freedom of the kitchen but we had to be careful where we walked because it could change the colour of it`s skin to suit the background. When placed on a tartan sheet it couldn`t cope and became angry. In the winter months it never strayed from the fireplace but one severe winter saw it off. I was very sad at its passing and I put it in a wooden box and buried it in the back garden.

We couldn't wait for Guy Fawkes night to set our fireworks off so on the night we had none left. In the following years we let off only a few of our fireworks before bonfire night because my Dad and Mr Holton from across the road said that they would organise a fireworks display in our backyard it being the biggest. Bobby's friends and their parents gathered there to see them. It was quite a spectacle.

Some familiar figures regularly to be seen trading their wares down the back lanes were the rag and bone men attracting attention by blowing a bugle. They would swap a bundle of rags or jam jars for a goldfish. I used to take jam jars to Logan's rag shop in Thomas St next to the school and I would get a penny for three empty jars,

men with a horse a cartload of coal selling coal slacks at a penny a stone, tuppence for roundies and fishwives shouting five a penny caller herring. In the front streets came the milkman pushing his handcart and selling milk from gills and pint measuring cans, the cutler with his big portable grinding wheel sharpening knives and scissors. A man selling matches, shoe and boot laces from a tray. Charlie Chuck see p40 was a well known character who wandered the streets playing his tin whistle was in the audience.

During the interval a volunteer was called for and he went up to the projecting room. A few minutes later his image was on the screen. Everyone thought that it was done by mirrors or some other form of trickery.

In September I started my first term of night classes at the Redby School in Fulwell Rd. learning Maths, Science and English. One night there was a brilliant show of the Northern Lights.

. For many years there were several magic lantern halls in town but they only showed still pictures with a narrator explaining the plot and a pianist supplying the sound effects. By the time I was old enough to go to these shows they were being ousted by the cinemas which were screening silent movies. I saw only a couple of slide shows in church halls. There were three local cinemas The Roker, Bromarsh and Cora, short for coronation also known as the Loppy House. The Cora had wooden forms in the cheap section and wooden seats in the posh end. In other parts of town were the Havelock, Kings, Palace, Gaiety, Villiers and the Picture House commonly known as the Ranch because most of the films shown were about cowboys and Indians or castle rustlers. We used to call them the goodies and the baddies. The Saturday matinees at the three local cinemas were known as the penny crush and were rowdy affairs. The show opened with a short film such as "Felix the cat" "The Cohens and the Kellys" followed by a weekly serial one being "The Perils of Pauline". Next came a preview of the following week's production.

Then came the main feature usually a western or adventure film. Some of the heroes were Tom Mix, Hoot Gibson, Bill Boyd and Ken Maynard.

Later when talking pictures replaced the silents the kids were still noisy and often when the villain was stalking the hero a child would cry out "Look out he is coming up behind you" and the cry was taken up by the rest of them and never let up until the lights were switched on. With the lights on it was difficult to see the images on the screen and it stayed that way until the noise abated. When the lights were put out they settled down but it wasn`t long before the noise started up again. It took a long time for them to learn how to be quiet at a talkies picture show.

The Roker cinema screened one of the first full length talking pictures to be shown in Sunderland. It was called "Daddy Long Legs" starring Charles Farrel and Janet Gaynor.

Dundas St was extensively used on August Bank Holiday Monday every year and from my window I would watch the procession of many Jazz bands and floats carrying entertainers as it passed by. It started from the East End and made its way through the town, over the bridge then down Dundas St, terminating on the Block Yard at Roker where steam organs were blasting out music, round-a-bouts, swings, switchbacks, dodge-em cars, stalls of roll a penny , bingo, horse racing, side shows exhibiting a bearded lady, a tattooed lady and others with hundreds of revellers jostling around, many clutching prizes they had won.

Being a child I wasn`t aware that the town was already in depression with most shipyards and other industries were either closed or working short time with the majority of men on the dole. Every day the police box at the Wheat Sheaf displayed the information that Wearmouth Pit would be idle that day or be open.

After a certain length of time an unemployed man had his dole stopped for six weeks then he went back on the dole. This period was known as the GAP. He then applied for public assistance which was a humiliating experience and a lot less money than dole.

A few months after moving to 5 Dundas St. Grays shipyard in Pallion closed down and my Dad got the chop and was out of work for six years. My Dad like thousands of other men was without a regular job for nearly six years and was forced on to the GAP. He suffered this indignity once and to avoid a repetition he took on work as a Public Works night watchman for low pay for short periods so as to accumulate sufficient stamps to qualify for dole. His hours of work 5-00pm till 7-30am for five nights then from Friday 5-00pm till Monday 7-30am non-stop all for 6d an hour.

After school often while Mam was out shopping I had tea with Dad and he told me stories about the Great War and some of his own exploits. One was when tunnelling toward the German trenches he could hear the Germans tunnelling parallel to his own.

About the same time as my Dad losing his job Uncle Harry was paid off from JL Thompson but found one at Burnt Island in Scotland. After working there for a few months he was offered a job in Middlesborough. When he had settled in his family joined him and they lived there for a couple of years. I went to stay with them for a month during the schools summer holidays. With my cousins and their friends we often played on some fenced off waste land. It reminded me of Blumers derelict shipyard where we were chased off a few times but were never caught. It was the same here.

Uncle Harry threatened to feed us to the nearby blast furnaces if any of us stepped out of line.

At night the flames were clearly visible from our bedroom window and we wondered how many naughty children were being burnt.

When Uncle Harry was offered the chance to return to JL Thompson he accepted and they came back to Sunderland and moved in with her sister Louise and her husband Alex Turner in Marlboro St. Millfield.

About 1933-4 Uncle Alex sold his shop and moved to Close St. and Aunt Bella moved to 28 Franklin St. both adresses in Millfield

BRIDGE OPENING CEREMONY

The original iron bridge over the River Wear was opened in the presence His Royal Highness the Duke of Gloucester on the 9th August 1796.

The re-construction of this bridge began in 1927 and never stopped the flow of traffic until the opening day 3rd October 1929 when his Royal Highness the Duke of York completed the work by hammering home a silver rivet. After dinner I went to see the Bridge Opening Ceremony which should have ended in time for me to get to school before the afternoon lesson began but it didn`t and I was late. My punishment was to stand at the teachers desk in front of the class and describe the scenes that I had seen.

On footall match days it was very difficult to walk against the hundreds of supporters returning home over the bridge to town. This became one of our play areas.

We would clamber up the top side of the arch framework then slide down. Go inside the boxed girders and climb up as far as we dared. I managed three parts of the way up. None of us came to grief.. Other areas we played in were the disused wharves, after the workmen had left for the day in Newcastle Rd swimming baths foundations under construction When it first opened to the public it boasted a spring board and a twenty foot high diving board. I remember many years later diving from this high board for the first time. I was winded and I weakly swam to the side and rested. I learned from the experience.

While playing at pirates and smugglers in the Holey Rock caves at Roker we were often caught by the incoming tide and had to plodge our way out. On several occasions boys who were strangers to this area not as experienced as us stayed inside too long and the lifeboat had to be called to rescue them.

Some days when at the North Dock I would watch the lock gates being opened by a couple of men laboriously turning a windlass by hand. When open a ship would slowly sail through and tie up at the Oil Terminal. The men would then close the gates. A similar manoeuvre would be made for a ship outward bound. When the lock gates were closed they formed a square inside with the trapped waters swirling round like whirlpool. When they were open anyone wishing to go to Greenwells, the North Eastern Marine Engine Works or the beach would have to wait or take the long walk round the perimeter of the square dock. Round about 1929 they fell into disuse and were left open and a thick broad wooden boom was securely placed across the entrance. It was probably meant to keep the dock free of rubbish but it served another purpose. Rather than walk round the dock the men chose to climb down the ladder to the boom and walk across it and climb up the other side then proceed to their destination.

It wasn`t that simple because after short time the boom was covered in moss and many a person slipped into the water. Eddie Patterson who lived just a few doors from me was much older than me and he seemed to be forever fishing men out of the dock after slipping from the boom.

1930

When a ship berthed at the Oil Terminal the seamen, some were foreign would go in a shed at the dock side and sit and talk. We sat beside them, sometimes we were brought into conversation with them and were never chased away. When the berth was empty we swam in the dock and dived from the raft.

Every year just before Xmas my Mam baked a few fruit loaves, one for us and the others for her married brothers and sisters. My role was to remove the stalks from the currents and raisins. When the mixture was put inside the fireside oven no one was allowed to enter or leave the room until it was baked and it usually took fours, perhaps longer. The speciality of the year was to have a goose for our Xmas dinner but before it could be cooked I had to pluck out the feathers. When that was done I held it while my Dad scorched the flesh with a red hot poker. This was to ensure that there were no quills left in the flesh.

During the festive season families and friends took turns to organise a party at home and for some years it fell to us to entertain them on New Year's Eve. The men went out to the nearest pub while the women stayed in and prepared a wonderful spread of pig's cheek, ham, tongue, goose and pickled onions to name just a few.

When the men returned most of us went down the street to Thompson's Memorial Hall for the watch night service to welcome in the New Year. While we were away Notarianni delivered a freezer of ice cream and the few at home were the first to sit down to a sumptuous meal. On our return we sat down for the second sitting. After the feast party games and dancing went on into the early hours. The guests would then start leaving and often had to trudge home in deep snow.

In the late 1920s the area around Seaside Lane became known as Seaburn and was made more attractive to the detriment of Roker. We did not desert it. It was closer to home.

I often went for my Mams messages in the following local shops. The Meadow Dairy, The Ryhope and Silksworth Co-op, The Maypole, Duncans and Catchpole for groceries. Parker for rabbits, fruit and vegetables and Allens the butcher for fresh meat where the floor was always covered with sawdust to soak up the blood. Hunter in Lower Dundas St had several shops each selling their own brand of goods. In addition there were Simmons sweet shop, Smith and Stephenson caterers, fried fish and chip shop, bric- brac, Douds the pork butcher, coffee shop and an ice-cream parlour.

Maggie Stevenson and Dick Watson were work friends of my Mam when she was single some years ago while serving for Sir James Nott at Wylam. They became lifelong friends and after they were married called at each others homes. When they called on us I played in the back yard garden with Dorothy their daughter who was about my age and son Richard who was much younger.

On football match days when Sunderland AFC home games were played on a Saturday and sometimes on a Wednesday at 3-00pm at their Roker Park ground motor cars used every possible street to make their way home and Dundas St. experienced an hour long cavalcade of cars.

HORSES TO CARS AND LORRIES

By 1930 horses had to a large extent given way to mechanised vehicles such as saloon cars, small vans and 30cwt lorries each one powered by a petrol engine. Motor traffic had increased immensely. Roker Avenue was still the main route from the town to Roker and South Shields by-passing Dundas St.

New models of lorries were being brought on to the roads and Vaux Brewery tried replacing the horse drays by first introducing a lorry without a petrol engine. This was powered by a steam engine with the coal-fired boiler mounted at the front. The glow from the fire heralded it`s approach during the dark nights.

In keeping with tradition only the horse drawn drays made deliveries to the local public houses and off-licences. More modern means of transport was used for other destinations. This continued right up to the late 1990s when the Vaux brewery closed down.

There were three depots where tram-cars were garaged when not in use, one in Hylton Rd at the top of Silksworth Row, the Fulwell Railway crossing and the Wheat Sheaf. When a tram ended its final run at the Wheat Sheaf, it moved along North Bridge St, turned into Dundas St, then into the back lane and into the tram shed. Around 1930 this entrance/exit was closed off and the trams now used the Wheat Sheaf entrance/exit only so making the tramlines in Dundas St redundant.

Most streets and back lanes in the town were laid with cobble-stones but this particular section of road had tarred wooden blocks. The disused tramlines were removed and so were the tarred blocks. Many of these found their way on to local kitchen fires. The road was then re-surfaced with tarmacadam.

After Easter the weather became warm and fine and it usually lasted till late Autumn.

During this period a party of my relatives and friends went to the Seaburn beach or boated on the river. The tides dictated which pursuit to be followed and when. With a rising tide we set off from the Wearmouth Bridge in a hired rowing boat and I often swam behind it for part of the way. We stopped at the Hylton Woods sometimes a little further up to Coxgreen then go ashore to have our sandwiches and to play games until the tide turned. On the following Sunday when the tide was flowing down to the sea we went to the beach. There were sand artists exercising their skills creating embossed pictures of cathedrals, castles, a horse and carriage and a street scene to name just a few. Alongside these artistic works lay a cloth cap to collect pennies from the onlookers. Buskers were in abundance playing musical instruments. For the children there were donkey rides for a penny. We hired deckchairs and a tent. One of the party had a pennant with the letters BYT. She said that the letters were for Belle Youngstones tent but nationally it meant Bright Young Things. This was fastened to the tent top and it was a good landmark.

It was easy to get lost there were so many tents on the sands. Most of the crowd swam or plodged in the sea. The games played were football, rounders, mount-a-kitty, cricket and leap frog. When exhausted we settled down to tea and sandwiches. To make the tea hot water was brought from a cafe on the sea front.

On the rare occasions when it rained everyone dashed to the big shelter on the Low Promenade. At the end of the day we all trooped off to my Aunt Frans house in Annie St to finish off the food.

1931

The blackberry week school holiday came much too late to pick them as the bushes were almost bare of berries. Instead we went taty gleaning. There were many farms on
the town boundaries where the farmers were harvesting their potato crops. Word spread around that gleaning would commence on a certain day at one farm or another.

Dozens of people would stand at the edge of the field waiting for the harvesting to start. The tractors ploughed the potatoes up and were put into a following cart by farmhands. When they were close to the end of the field the farmer gave the signal for people to start. The potatoes overlooked by the farmhands were picked up by the advancing gleaners. When my bag was full I took it home and when I emptied the bag a cabbage fell out. I wonder how that came to be there ?.

My Grandda Bell died after months of suffering from water filling his legs. Uncle John my Dads brother an outside manager for Brentford Gasworks lived in 72 Silver Crescent Chiswick London. He came up for the funeral and stayed with us for a few days.

During summer holidays an evangelist set up a platform on the Roker sands and named it Sunshine Corner. His name was William Harvey and to the children he was Uncle Will and he encouraged them to come on the platform to sing hyms either solo, duo or in groups. He commanded a large following of children and adults. He always began his service with this song "Sunshine Corner"and everyone joined in.

Sunshine Corner oh its mighty fine
Its for children under ninety-nine
All our welcome seats are given free
Roker Sunshine Corner is the place for me

I had been a wolf cub for a couple of years at Dock St Chapel and it was time to move into the scouts but there was not a troop here. Whitburn Chapel and ours had only just amalgamated so I joined their Boys Brigade where I learned first-aid, semaphore, knots and the bugle. I gained certificates and badges for first-aid. The commanding officers were Captain Watson and Lieutenant Downs. Our uniform consisted of a black forage cap with two narrow parallel strips of white linen round the two sides and a metal number 2 pinned on it. A leather belt with the logo "Sure and Steadfast" on the buckle and a white linen haversack. All linen had to be blancoed before attending the weekly meetings and the church parades. One of the highlights of my childhood was taking part in the Boys Brigade Jubilee in Glasgow with companies from all over the world in 1933.

A territorial army bugler the holder of the silver bugle award taught us to play the bugle.

Once a month on Sunday mornings we met at the Roker Park football ground. We formed fours then to the music of the bugles and kettledrums we marched to Whitburn St Chapel. After the service we again formed fours then were dismissed. In the afternoon I attended Dock St Chapel Sunday School.

Mr Turnbull was the leader of the Gloopers club named after Gloops a cat in a comic strip in the "Evening World" newspaper.

We received a tea-set in exchange for the "Evening World" serial numbers saved over a number weeks. All sorts of crafts were being taught and one summer day we all went to Seaburn.

The old North Pier was crumbling and only the lighthouse and its flashing warning light were being maintained. At low tide we sometimes played among the rotting timbers or watched the men fishing. An occasional water-rat would come out of the sea and run around the foundations scaring us to death. At the turn of the tide the level of the river began to rise and lapped at our feet. It was time for everyone to move. The fishermen climbed to higher beams to continue fishing. We went to the top decking to play then later down the stone buttress to the bathing sands and played till home-time.

A change in the education system resulted in me and all the other ten year olds being transferred to Thomas St School near the Wheat Sheaf clock and pub. We were taught fractions and the metric system and one day Mr Prince the Headmaster came to see how we were getting on. He was pleased with us and then he wrote the letter X on the blackboard and he asked us what it meant. Trying to impress we said it was the Roman number ten. He told us that it was correct but it also had another meaning and then went on to unfold some of the mysteries of algebra. Mr Etherington a teacher of another class was the brother of my school friend Bob Etherington. My teacher Mr Mountford had served in France and Belgium with my Dad in 1916 had been wounded but not as bad as my Dad who had lost an arm. One of his wrists had a scar from a bullet wound. He taught us arithmetic, geometry, geography, history and grammar. Set in the wall above the front door of a house directly opposite to the school gate was a sun-dial.

When a lesson was held in the school-yard the teacher would ask us what the time was and we had to answer using roman numerals.

We went to Raby Castle one day on a school trip. We enjoyed it, one reason being we missed the English grammar and poetry lesson.

There was a school camp in Seaham where in summer deprived children were sent free for a week. Only one boy bare footed in my class qualified.

A church in Middleton in Teesdale had been converted into a camp for Sunderland school children. It was not free. For the same purpose a collection of huts was used at Seaburn.

1932

At week-ends and holidays we walked to the Tunstall Hills, Hylton Woods or Boldon Flats where we searched for frogs, tadpoles and newts.

The government introduced a land settlement scheme to help the unemployed. Many of out of work miners of whom my Uncle George Forth was one took advantage of the scheme. They took their families to the South of England and my Uncle George with his family settled on a plot of land in Siddlesham Sussex.

My Mam, Dad, brother Bob and Me went to Silksworth one night to see them on their way. Their furniture had gone ahead of them and the house was bare with only the coal fire almost burned out. The bus arrived, Uncle locked up and gave up the keys. They boarded the bus now filled with families all waving as it pulled away on the long night journey to the South.

1933

After eighteen months at Thomas St School terminating in 1933 I returned to Stansfield St Senior Boys School. It was around this time that the National School near JL Thompsons shipyard was closed and many pupils were transferred to my school. Andrew Wyness and Bartholomew Hutchinson were two of those who came into my class bringing the number of boys to nearly fifty. Once a week those who were interested went to the High St baths for swimming lessons. Leaving the school we walked in a single file to the Wearmouth Bridge crossed over then turned right into Matlock St and were greeted with an aroma from a sweet factory. Stopping at the open gate we watched the men and girls at machines stretching the mixture of sugar and Glucose before it was turned into sticks of candy rock. Reluctantly leaving the pleasant sweet smelling air behind us we walked by the Vaux Brewery and the aroma changed to that of Hops and on reaching the baths to Chlorine. In the baths I learned to swim and dive. I gained 3rd, 2nd, 1st certificates and a special. For this one I had to swim 440 yards without pause.

In the 1970s when the Crowtree Leisure Centre was opened the High St Baths were closed and eventually demolished. The entrance facade was saved and now graces the entrance to the Inland Revenue office built on the same site and still in business in 2011.

SUNDERLAND SCHOOLS FESTIVAL

All the schools in Sunderland were preparing displays for a festival to be held in the Roker Park football ground. Our school fielded a team of sword dancers, not the highland version dancing over crossed swords but a dance having several set pieces. Our class teacher Taffy Watson was also our choreographer. There were eight of us in the team. We stood in a line each boy holding the sword held by the boy in front just like a line of circus elephants.

Following the leader we weaved in and out and as we snaked along done a tricky routine. Four pairs fought mock duals. The climax was at the end when we formed a circle and thrust our swords into the centre where they interlocked and took on the shape of circular badge which the leader held above his head.

Once a week we walked to the Jeffrey Hall in Monk St near the Wheat Sheaf. We done an hour physical training PT. swinging dumbells and Indian clubs, vaulting over a wooden horse, jumping over a bar at increasing heights. I dont remember what the height was when I knocked it down.

I played in the schools rugby team and when playing against Monkwearmouth Central School I came up against Walter Knox see p39, 87 their full back with whom I was to meet again in the near future. Taffy Watson was our rugby coach. The fixture games were played on Saturday mornings on a home and away basis. Our home ground was on the Seaburn Camp playing fields. The away games were played at Plains Farm, Sparks Farm, Holmes Farm, Tunstall Hills and Grangetown.

My first visit to a school camp was located in a farmers field in Leamside near Finchale Priory and Mr Jollie was in charge. At the end of the first day an initiating ceremony was organised and was held at midnight. First timers to the school camp were to stay in their tents until called. Meanwhile Mr Jollie the interrogator and those pupils who had been through it before were the ghosts and they laid a tarpaulin sheet on the ground. I was one of those waiting in a tent. When my name was called I was made to kneel down on the sheet and to answer a number of questions. Suddenly the sheet was whisked sharply away. Bring on the next victim. You may guess the rest. There was plenty to do every day. Sunbathing, swimming in the river, picking wild raspberries on the river bank just below the camp site, walks to Finchale Abbey, paperchases, football, cricket and train rides to Durham and visits to the cathedral. Each boy worked in the field kitchen for one whole day, fetching, carrying, washing up, helping with the cooking and keeping the area tidy. On the last night we had a beano and a singsong sitting around the camp fire.

At playtime we swapped paper backs. They were the Adventure, Wizard, Rover, Hotspur and Skipper. The comics were the Rainbow, Tiger Tim, Comic Cuts and Radio Fun. We were banned from reading these papers in our Friday afternoon freetime class. Looking back I believe that I had learned a lot from them. Although fictional the stories were based on real life adventures in both geographical and historical settings.

We also collected and swapped cigarette cards another source of useful information the Jubilee of King George V, speed, warships of the world, make do and mend, cathedrals, castles, regiments, flags and many more. All were lost in the passing of time.

Every Wednesday afternoon after school when Sunderland was playing at home we went to the Roker Park AFC football ground at the end of the street and waited until ten minutes before the end of the game when the large gates were opened to allow the crowds to leave the ground quickly. A fleet of tram-cars was waiting near to the ground ready to take passengers to the town centre. We went in and sometimes were lucky to see a goal scored. One Wednesday a cup-tie was played against Derby County and a crowd of more than 75,000 attended and we were kept back at school preventing us from going to the ground. It was for our own safety but we did not appreciate that at the time.

We had the choice of reading in class or going to the Seaburn school playing fields for our Friday freetime lesson. I chose to go to the field.

We walked from the school and on reaching the Mere Knolls Cemetery gate we followed the path outside of the cemetery wall with the golf course on our right keeping our eyes open for lost golf balls. A golfer would give a penny for any ball found.

I was twelve years old when I bought my first bike on the never never at sixpence a week over two years. It was a Hercules model, sit up and beg type. My first ride was to South Shields and back. Next rides were to Durham and Newastle.

On these rides I passed many smoking pit heaps and I let my imagination run riot.

They were volanoes. Some Sunday mornings I followed a cycling club on their rides but after a short time I was left behind. They rode racing bikes and I was unable to keep pace with them. However over the next year or two I went as far as Barnard Castle, Stockton and Morpeth.

The Houghton Cut was very steep, long and straight and at the bottom into Houghton-le-Spring passing the church and into the High St. I have ridden my bike from the bottom of the cut to the top no more than a dozen times. It was a real challenge. Most times I had to dismount and wheel it to the top. Some years after World War Two ended the top of the cut was lopped off and the road is now about twenty feet lower.

One day I rode to Roker and there waited for the White Star Passenger Liner Olympic to pass the New North Pier lighthouse on its way to Hebburn on the Tyne to be broken up. When it came into view I kept pace with it as it sailed along the coast. It stopped at South Shields to pick up the river pilot. I then followed it up river. After it was safely tied up I made my way home. A few days later the ship was opened to the public and I rode direct to the yard one day and spent a couple of hours exploring the decks and the interior but what I wanted to see was barred to the public. They were the engine and boiler rooms.. Another day I cycled to Dunstan on the River Tyne to visit my Uncle Dave on his ship SS Hindustan. I stayed longer than I had intended and it was turning dark as I rode through Gateshead. I was stopped by a

policeman who advised me to walk through built up areas to avoid being stopped again and perhaps being booked for riding without a light. Because of this my Uncle Billy gave me two paraffin oil lamps and were used until 1937 when I was able to buy battery operated cycle lamps.

Tommy Cuthbertson a school friend who lived in my street rode on his bike to school and on occasions when I left home late after dinner he took me to school on the crossbar.

A DOUBLE WEDDING

Vin Skeen was courting my Aunt Hilda and Uncle Jim was courting Margaret Aiken and both men were working at Dunston power station and travelled together on a motorbike and sidecar. The foursome decided to be married in a double wedding ceremony in Venerable Bede Church in Newcastle Rd near the Wheat Sheaf. My young brother Bobby was to be their page-boy but a few days before the wedding date he went down with chicken pox so until after the wedding I was packed off to live with my Grandma and Grandda Blenkinsop.

The reception was in the Boilermakers Arms, High St in the town centre. While the grown ups were in the hall dancing us children were playing on the stairs landing. One of the girls tumbled down the stairs and broke an arm. Both couples went to live in the same house in Bede St Roker.

Some months later Uncle Vin was paid off and he found a job in Peterborough. Uncle Vin and Aunt Hilda moved to Peterborough and our attic play room was used to store their furniture. A couple of years later he got a job at Doxfords and they came back to Cecil St in Millfield and we got our attic play room back.

About the same time we often accompanied Uncle George Bell a sergeant in the Durham Light Infantry DLI to the drill hall in Livingstone Rd to watch boxing matches and visit the firing range. My Dad was a good shot even though he only had one arm the other was shot off in the battle for Vimy Ridge on Easter Monday 1917.

I mixed in with the army cadets cleaning rifles and learning some of their activities. I wanted to join but my parents were against the idea.

The drill hall was used to hold dances and members from both of our families attended. I remember playing with Sergeant Carrols little girl and being a bit of a nuisance amongst the dancers.

1934

At Easter time a fun fair was held in the garrison field and like those held on the Block Yard, Southwick Oval and the Town Moor there were plenty of amusements, rides and sideshows.

From the steam engines music was being blasted out by steam being blown through correctly spaced punched holes in a roll of paper. It was very loud and was heard from a long way off.

On Easter Sunday I visited Grandma and Aunties with my two cousins to collect chocolate eggs some with our names written on them with white icing and paste eggs painted in bright colours.

Like last year this summer school camp was held in the same Leamside field. Mr Jollie was in charge once again. A student teacher Gus Gardner was here to help him. As in the previous year an initiating ceremony was held. This time I was one of the ghosts initiating the newcomers and the events being similar to last years event ensured that a good time was had by all.

In the Autumn a battleship the HMS Valiant visited Sunderland. Because it was too big to enter the river it lay just beyond the New North Pier. In the town sailors were to be seen everywhere. Visitors were welcomed aboard and dozens of crafts of all sizes were brought into service to ferry the many hundreds of people to the ship.

It was my bad luck on reaching the battleship to find that it was chock full of people and no more were allowed to board her that day and we had to be content with a slow trip round the vessel before going back to the dock. It was brilliantly lit up at night and the searchlights swept over the sea and foreshore.

The towns sewage system was being extended to Roker and came out at the Roker Park exit at the beach. The sands were about five or six feet lower down and a trestle bridge was being built to support the drain pipe. While under construction children from all parts would play on the site after the workmen had gone home. One night one of our school friends Billy Bell, not related to me, while playing on the timber scaffolding fell and was killed.

We often played outside of the Derby pub at the bottom of our block and at the top the Albion. The Albion survived the 1960s redevelopment of the area and is still flourishing today in 2009.

The surrounding streets and the Derby pub were all demolished and high rise flats and bungalows were built on the land. A new Derby pub was built near Roker Park football ground.

Another pastime was to climb over the Millum Terrace wall, stand on the ledge on its other side and then jump over the space on to the level top of the gentlemen's convenience, shin down then repeat.

Single decker electric tramcars displaced horses as early as 1900 and were powered by overhead cables. A trailing jib on the roof of the tram was used to conduct electricity to the motor which motivated the tram. When in motion sparks were emitted where the jib roller contacted the cable. At the terminus this jib had to be reversed. When I was at a terminus I watched the conductor swing the jib round by using a long pole which when not in use was rested at the side of the tram. Efforts to eliminate sparking led to a pantograph frame being fitted with a reversible contact, the pole now no longer needed. This remained in use until trams were dispensed with. When double decker buses were introduced only the Villette Rd/Southwick route retained single decked trams because at a few hundred feet apart were two low railway bridges over Hendon Rd. In later years I recall at least one double decker with no passengers going back to the depot taking a short cut attempted to pass under a bridge and its roof was torn off.

My Uncle Bill had a bivouac and he often camped at Leamside. To save carrying it backwards and forwards he left it in the farmers barn. On a few occasions I borrowed it and camped there with a friend.

I was now thirteen and my time to be back home was extended to ten-thirty. Mr Coulson who lived in Millum Terrace just around the corner to Dock St East owned a motor bike and sidecar. The only times I ever saw it on the road were on some nights at nine he would bring his combination out and drive it to the Derby pub about two hundred yards away then enter the pub. Just after closing time at ten he drove it home and put it away.

Radio broadcasting had improved and my Dad bought a wireless complete with a loudspeaker from Brechner shop in Crowtree Rd in the town centre. The wireless was powered by two batteries 20volts and 9volts each lasting about six months and an accumulator which had to be charged up every few days and Mr Jameson at the bottom of our street made a business of re-charging accumulators and it was a common sight to see people carrying a one to or from his shop. He also hired out hand-carts at 6d per hour. My uncles used them to deliver furniture to customers homes

When the new rugby season began I signed up with Cragside a local rugby club and played on Saturday afternoons after school rugby on the morning. A committee of club secretaries divided all the clubs into two sections, North Sunderland and South Sunderland. Every few weeks a friendly would be played between the North and the South. I was chosen to play for the North in a few of the games.

1935

A cycle ride to remember. I missed this years Good Friday march see p42 to go with George Holmes a school friend on a cycling visit to his Uncle and Aunt who lived on a hillside in Eastgate.

It was a warm morning and the sun was shining when we set off and riding through the town we passed hundreds of marching scholars.

After passing them we made good progress until we reached Wolsingham where it had been snowing.

The snowploughs had swept the roads clear and both sides of the road were piled high with snow. Nearing Eastgate it began to snow and the going became heavy. Arriving at his Aunties cottage we were welcomed in and put before a roaring coal fire and given a hot meal. We stayed till nine then left for home. It snowed all the way and with no street lights between the built up areas we had a rough journey. When we reached the town boundary we saw that Sunderland had not escaped. We arrived home at 3-00am all wet and cold.

This year my third school camp was to be held just outside of Hexham with Mr Jollie in charge again. When he was studying in Cologne University he was courting a German girl and this summer she and her brother Ernst Wilmes were in Sunderland and Ernst was to come camping with us. Some weeks beforehand Mr Jollie had told us about the German lad and warned us not to goose-step or make NAZI salutes which we had all been doing for the last few months. He taught us a few German phrases, the German national anthem and a hymn, some I still remember. We were not too sure what to expect of the German lad but after we had met I found him to be a likeable person. He was tall blond and athletic and he may have been in the Hitler Youth Movement but nothing of that nature was ever brought up. We had a great time learning some of the games he played in Germany.

In that year or maybe the previous one the German Graf zeppelin on a courtsey visit hovered over our school which is not far from the docks.

All the children were brought from their classrooms into the school yard to see it. I thought about this visit years later when during an air raid on the town the Monsanto oil tanks on the North Dock were blown up. After the war I met Mr Jollie in the town and he told me that his German girl friend had died in an air raid on Cologne. He was then Headmaster at the Bede Grammer School. In my last term at school Mr Jollie was put in charge of all pupils having successfully completed the curriculum and he was welcomed by all of us. We had already learned fractions, algebra, decimals and the metric system and he was now going to teach us the basics of logarithms, French and various scientific subjects. In the science lessons he used a magic lantern illuminated by a phosphorous tablet which was always difficult to get burning. This and many other different experiments he conducted earned him the nickname "The Mad Scientist" which we used in a complimentary manner. He explained how executions were done in America and then organised a practical demonstration. Every boy held the hand of each boy sitting on either side of him. The boys at both ends of the line with their free hand held a length of cable connected to a positive terminal and negative.

When Mr Jollie closed the switch it completed the circuit and a mild charge of electricity surged through our bodies. He then explained that in a real execution thousands volts were applied.

This year another battleship the HMS Malaya arrived on a courtsey visit and it too lay just beyond the New North Pier. I was lucky this time. I was able to spend several hours on board exploring all departments except the engine and boiler rooms which were out of bounds to all visitors.

Like the HMS Valient it was brilliantly lit up with the searchlights sweeping across the East End, Monkwearmouth, Roker and Seaburn every night.

The sailors were welcomed in the dance halls and the pubs. In the streets young girls ran up to a sailor to touch his collar.

My fourteenth birthday was in the middle of my last term at school and I began to think of looking for a job. I was interested in two classes of work. One choice was to be an engine fitter so that I could go to sea as an engineer. My second was to be a woodworker because in the last year or two I became interested in making useful wooden articles.

After finding the names and addresses of several firms likely to engage mechanical fitters or joiners I began my seach for work. I set off on my bike every day at 6-300am searching and then be at school for 9-00am. It was very dark at this time of year on the roads. The street lamps were widely spaced and only cast a feeble light and my paraffin lamps were no better. A year on I replaced them with two battery operated lamps. When looking for work on arriving at any one the shipyards, engine works. foundries, joiner shops and builders yards I awaited the arrival of the foreman and told him that I was looking for an apprenticeship. They would tell me that there was nothing doing at the present time but come and try again.

A school open day was arranged for parents to come and see their children doing their class work. Preparations for this day were being made by Mr Jollie teaching us various skills. On Open Day all classes but ours were to carry on with lessons as normal but the pupils in our class were to demonstrate the practicle skills that we had learned. At last the day dawned and we were all excited and nervous as we awaited the arrival of our parents. When we saw that the visitors were showing real interest we settled down and the classroom became a hive of industry, every boy doing his own thing. My task was glass blowing. The good articles that I had made while learning the art lay on the table beside me. Parents watched as I created small ornaments which were given away. It was a successful veventure.

On the last day of term we were told that we may return to school after the Xmas and New Year holday if we had not found a job.

CHAPTER 3

1936 TO 1939

In January most of us returned to continue our education. We were then informed that we were free to come and go in search of employment. One by one a boy would arrive late in the day and say that he had found a job.

In my quest for work I tried for an apprenticeship with Coutes and Findlaters shopfitters in Hudson Rd. Binns joiners in Crowtree Rd, Doxford joiner shop in Pallion and Ranken the Builder in Park Lane.

On the engineering side there were the Wear Winch Foundry in Park Lane, Jennings Foundry in Tatham St, Doxford Engine Works Pallion and Austin below the Wearmouth Bridge and then came mixed fortunes. Once again I tried the Wear Winch on the last Saturday in January. This time the foreman told me to come and start work on Monday at 7-30am.

That afternoon my Mam took me to town and had me fitted out with overalls and work boots.

On the Monday dressed in my new brown overalls I cycled to my first job with my sandwiches wrapped in a red and white spotted hankerchief slung from the handlebars. I was so excited that I arrived early. When the foreman turned up he took me to the moulding shop and said that it was here where I would learn to be a moulder. I was disappointed to hear that and I told him that what I wanted was to be a fitter not a moulder and I could not accept this job.

After thanking him for the chance I left and cycled furiously to the Doxford Engine Works and was just in time to catch Mr Wilson the foreman coming through the gates and I immediately attracted his attention.

I told him where I had been earlier and why I had decided not to take that job after all. After a few questions he told me to come back next day and report for work at the Time Office at 7-05am and ask for Mr Mathews or Mr Johnston. Either of them would give me a time card and instructios. Thanking him I raced home to tell my parents and young brother my good news and then to school to tell Mr Jollie and Mr Craggs the Headmaster who gave me a written reference which I used to advantage in future years. After saying goodbye to my classmates I went home bubbling over with excitement. At this time less than one third of the boys had found a job. Many years later I learned that one of them Frank Dodsworth had become a moulder at the Wear Winch Foundry in Park Lane and I wondered if he had taken the job that I had passed over.

MY FIRST DAY AT WORK

The next day was Tuesday 28 January 1936 my first day at work which was to be a memorable one for me and for millions of people all over the world.

My first day at work began like this:-

I arrived at 7-05am and Mr Mathews gave me the conditions of employment. I was to work in the stores and the other parts of the works until I was sixteen when I would begin my apprenticeship proper. My working week of forty-seven hours over five and a half days Monday to Friday 7-300am till 5-00pm stopping for lunch12 noon till 1-00pm and Saturday 7-30am till 12noon. Weekly wage starting at four shillings four pence and three farthings before offtakes. Your take home pay will be about 4s-0d. There will be an increase in wages on every birthday till the end of your apprenticeship.

I clocked in and went to the engine works store where I met Mr Dean the storekeeper and the five lads I was to work with Tommy O`Brian, Tommy Crowe, Bobby Wood, Robert Taylor, and Charlie Staincliffe. When a vacancy in the fitting or machine shop arose a boy would leave the store.

Narrow corridors separated the columns of cupboards which held all sorts of spares which we handed over to any worker giving us an order chit. At the back of the store was a large box of Sal Volatile salts. Above the box was a small cupboard fixed to the wall. We sat on this box while watching the window for customers and we took turns serving them. When Mr Storey the head storekeeper left his office to come into the store we all jumped up and looked buay. The same applied if any other person in authority came in.

Very early in the morning while I was at the window serving a customer the lads balanced a can lid full of water on the slightly open cupboard doors. When I returned and sat against the doors they closed and the water spilled over me. Like all new starters I had been initiated.

At 11-30am the men trooped out of the workshops and by noon the only people left were the manager, foremen and apprentices. At noon we were sent home and the reason for the walk out was because the men wanted to go home and listen to the funeral of King George V which was to be broadcast to the world on the BBC radio that afternoon. Television hadn`t reached the North-East yet.

For book keeping reasons the working week began on a Wednesday and ended on a Tuesday.which meant that I had only been at work four and a half hours that week and on Saturday I received my first pay of three old pennies equal to 2.5 new pence.

Two weeks later Tommy O`Brian was transferred into the machine shop and fourteen year old Billy Francis came to work in the stores with us. There were three duties to be performed on Saturday mornings. Three boys with Mr Dean the storekeeper to look after the big store. Two boys would visit the foremans office in each of the machine, erecting, oil engine, funnel, blacksmith, tinsmith, plumbers, pattern maker, fitting out quay and the general office and leave a clean face towel in each and take the soiled ones away for laundering. Leaving the general office we always slid down the banister. One day we slid down into the arms of the General Manager. Another boy was to look after the oilstore. One day when it was my turn an apprentice from another department came for rags and oil. He was Walter Knox see p30, 87 and I had played against him in school rugby.

Uncle Vin was now working at Doxford after returning home from Peterborough and for a few months I went with him to 7 Percival St where Aunt Hilda prepared and served dinner for us all.

I gauged the time it took me to travel on my bike to and from work and after a few months decided to try going home for dinner. I varied my route sometimes over the Wearmouth Bridge, through the town, Trimdon St Doxford., other times Southwick, over Alexandria Bridge, Doxford. Both distances were about equal but traffic congestion varied and experience taught me which route to follow and when. There were occasions when I was forced to use the bus. Brakes to renew, a puncture or very bad weather. The bus service was not very good.

The main workforce at Doxford engine works and Shorts shipyard finished work at 5-00pm and the men huffed and puffed their way up their respective bank to the bus stop. Often it was after 5-30pm before the last of the men got on a bus. I sometimes made it but like most cyclists I was forced to dismount before reaching the top. What was very noticable when leaving the works at

5-00pm was the number of children at the gates asking the workmen for any bait they may have left.

When I was fifteen I left the stores to work a mechanical saw beside two grown men Alfie Bowen and Bobby Oswald whose job was to grind stauncheons. I then moved into the main machine shop learning the Shaper and Planer then until sixteen on a capstan lathe and I made friends with Tommy Lanagan and we worked together quite well. One day we had a difference of opinion and we tried to settle it with fisticuffs among the machines and for our pains were sacked on the spot. The sackings were changed to a few days suspension. A lesson learned. We remained friends and we both completed our apprenticeship. I believe that Tommy became a foreman and stayed with Doxford until it closed. I followed a different path which I believed to be much more adventurous and exciting.

Experiments with the street lighting were being carried out on the recently completed promenade at Seaside Lane. We often paraded along here and I thought that peoples faces under those lights looked ghastly.

The Avenue cinema in Gill Bridge Avenue was where I saw my first television picture although I did not realise it at the time. A well known character Charlie Chuck see p20 was in the audience.

During the interval a volunteer was called for and he went up to the projection room.. A few minutes later his image was on the screen. Everyone thought it was done by mirrors or some form of trickery.

In September I started my first term of night classes at the Redby School in Fulwell Rd. learning Maths, Science and English.

One night there was a brilliant show of the Northern Lights.

The lad I sat with was Leslie Blakeman an Apprenticed Industrial Chemist at Wearmouth Colliery. He was called to the colours in 1940 and served in the 125 anti-tank regiment and died in a Japanese prisoner of war camp A plaque with his name and others can be seen in the enntrance hall of the City Library in Fawcett St.

Every Xmas the Doxford workmen organised a social evening evening which was held in the Co-operative Hall in Green St. Tickets cost sixpence. In preparation for this social Molly and Isobel tried to teach me to dance. Uncle Harry didn`t help me very mush when he said that I had two left feet. I also listened to Victor Silvestor dancing lessons on the wireless. Other dance bands I listened to were Henry Hall, Jack Payne, Lew Stone and just for the music the Palm Court Orchestra. I followed up by going to Professor Dorn Dancing School in the YWCA in Burdon Rd. with Billy Richardson a friend from the Sunday School. Lessons were held every Friday night costing one shilling.

We had a lot of fun learning to dance and making friends. On leaving the hall we were given a concessionary ticket to the value of sixpence.

Next evening Saturday with this ticket and sixpence gains admission to the Alexandra Dance Hall (the Alex) on the top floor of the Victoria Hall.

1937

We developed into a large group of young boys and girls, Billy Richardson, Betty Watson, Reenee Watts, Maurice Snowball, Billy Glendenning, Ruth Rush, Joyce Wright, Ruth Willis, Mary Booth, Nancy Wake, Doreen Samson, Mary Samson, Eddie Neale, Barbara Wallace. Billy Richardson and myself visited the various dance halls in the town during the dancing season. Ruth Willis went to work in Southall, London. When she came home for holidays I dated her a few times. The winter was the season for dancing, summer for roller skating in the New Rink and to protect the dance floor a temporary floor was laid on top. It was here where I learned to dance on roller skates partnering Kitty Giblin.

On occasions the portable floor would be removed to allow a private dance to be held. Around June the Police Annual Ball was held one Wednesday evening from 7-30pm till 3-00am and I went with my cousin Isabel. Taking a girl to a dance on my own even though she is my cousin made me feel very much grown up. I took her home to Millfield after the dance then back to mine in Monkwearmouth. That was not so good as there was little time left for sleep before starting work at 7-30am.

Usually on a Saturday night Billy and me would meet in town and have a tuppenny pie at the Betta Pie shop next door to the Palace cinema in High St W. before deciding which dance hall we should visit. Very often it would be the Alex or the Marie Louise next door. Most of our crowd would be in one or the other. Other dance halls that we frequented were Masonic Hall and Morrison in North Bridge St, Jeffrey Hall Monk St, Binns recreation hut Newcastle Rd, Millfield Assembly Rooms Hylton Rd, New Rink Holmside, Co-operative Hall Green St.

Social evenings which were in effect dances were held in the church halls of St Peter and St Benet in Monkwearmouth, St Mark Millfield and Bishopwearmouth.

This was the year that Sunderland won the FA Cup.

Wilf Miller, Billy Richardson, Ronnie Francis and myself joined the bible class in Dock St Chapel. We also helped in monitoring the younger chidren in the Sunday School and pumping the bellows for the organ.

41

Some of the girls I remember are the three Robson sisters, Florence Littlefair, Mary Kent and May Stubbs. The boys Billy Richardson, Sammy Samuelson, Ben Locke, Tommy Dodsworth and Billy Maskell.

Sammy unable to find work here went to Northampton and found a job in the boot and shoe industry. After Chapel we often visited the Museum and the Winter Gardens. We then walked up Holmside, along Crowtree Rd, down High St West and along Fawcett St. Before going home we would do this circuit a few times along with dozens of other lads all walking the same way and droves of girls walking in the opposite direction. Many courtships sprang up from this boy meets girl situation.

Easter week-ends were nearly always warm and fine enough for the scholars of the local Sunday Schools to march from their own chapels to congregate around the Town Hall in Fawcett St. on Good Friday morning I marched with them most years missing 1935. see p34 Even Bridge St was packed solid with scholars and their teachers.

After the open service the marchers returned to their own chapels for a short service and on leaving were given an orange.

It was summer and jobs were still hard to find in this part of the country so my Dad hoping to find work in the south of the country hitched a lift on one Magogs furniture removal vans going beyond London. He stayed with his sister Maggie and family for a few weeks in Siddlesham. While he was there I travelled by bus and had a week holiday with them. I believe this was the first year that shipyard and engineering workers were given a week off with pay.

Their house was on a plot of land with a greenhouse filled with tomato plants and a battery of hens producing eggs daily and a patch growing flowers and vegetables and a nanny goat.

My Dad having only one arm was at a disadvantage when looking for work so without finding a job he retuned home with me at the end of my stay.

By September I had become moderate ballroom dancer and I was also pretty good at dancing on roller skates. On Saturday nights most people dancing at Wetheralls were over twenty-one and all under that age found it difficult to mix socially with them. We gave up after a couple of visits. In the work place we suffered the same alienation. At break times the men sat in groups or stayed on their own. The apprentices did likewise and never sat with their elders. It was common practice for the men to invite a lad completing his apprenticeship to sit with them. I came of age on 21 October 1942 but feeling no different from the day before I declined and continued to sit with my mates.

In those days most people were very superstitious and naive. One night a rumour swept through the town that a ghost had been seen in Green St and crowds flocked there to see it. I was one of them

Needless to say we were all disappointed. It did not show itself. Every Thursday night I would stay and look after the house while Mam and Dad were out. One night I heard a number of thumps coming from the landing. By the time I crossed the room and opened the door the thumps had stopped..

This was repeated at the same time each week.

This time when Mam and Dad returned home I told them about the thumps and my Mam said that it must be Annie coming to see that everything was alright and changed the subject. Annie was the previous tenant now deceased. The thumps continued for two or three more weeks then ceased altogether. I was almost convinced that the house was haunted but at night school I was learning that there was a logical reason for all actions including phenomenon but several years went before I learned the answer of the thumps see p18, 54.

At sixteen I was eligible to join a panel of doctors. Living above Doctor Hamiltons surgery what could be more natural than to register with him?

After a year at work I thought about converting an attic into a bedroom. I papered the walls and whitewashed the ceiling. A secondhand bed and dressing table were bought. The bed inside of the sideboard was folded up and its doors closed and the front room was returned to its former mode.

I had turned sixteen when Alan Aflecks cousin Maud Mushens see p76 came to stay with them for a holiday. During this time I saw a lot of her and we developed a puppy love crush toward one another. When she returned home we wrote letters to each other for some time.

1938

I got rid of my sit up and beg and replaced it with a semi-racing bike. It was fitted with a Sturmy Archer three speed gear, a mileometer and a dynamo feeding front and rear lights. My rides were now extended as far as Stockton, Barnard Castle and Whitley Bay.

THE GIRL I WAS TO MARRY

The East end of the town had a reputation for being a tough area. The police always patrolled there in pairs. There were two ways to reach the East End from Monkwearmouth.

Cross the river in the ferryboat or go over the Wearmouth Bridge and down the High St. As a boy I had only been there in the daytime never venturing after dark because of the warnings given about such visits and I wondered what it was really like. Now at seventeen I decided to have a look at it for myself. One night after dark I walked to Mackies corner, turned left into High St. which I believe was dimly lit by gas lamps. Going down the bank passing the New Arcade and Liverpool House I began to suffer from butterflies in the stomach and felt uneasy but I need not have worried. In the area I only saw jostling humanity..

At the bottom of the street I arrived at the Gaiety cinema, the Fish Quay and the Old Market. I went in the market which was illuminated by gas light and paraffin oil lamps. It was smoky. gloomy and noisy. There were stalls where furniture, kitchen ware, clothing, fruit, vegetables and all sorts of other stuff was being offered for sale. I walked past them all and came upon a fun fair the only part of the market with electricity used to operate the shuggy boats, round-a-bouts, swings and to light up the coconut shy, roll a penny and bingo stalls.

There was an entrance/exit to Coronation St. but not knowing where Coronation St led to I retraced my steps to the High St. Leaving the market I saw that the pubs were starting to fill up and I thought that the troubles I had been warned of perhaps started in them. However I was too young to enter them.

While walking along these streets and in the market I may even have rubbed shoulders with the girl I was to marry. She lived and worked in the area at the time. I must have spent a couple of hours in the area and never heard a wrong word or saw any signs of a disturbance. This experience helped to prepare me for when I was to travel to some of the worlds so called dodgy ports in later years.

One classic event at the fun fair held on the Town Moor was of a man astride a bike on a platform on top of a very high tower. He rode the bike over the edge and plunged into a small tank of water only four feet deep. He emerged unhurt.

Grandma Bell died due to the flame in the gas oven being blown out while cooking a meal. To enable Dads sisters Maggie from Siddlesham and Ciss from Arundel to stay with us for the funeral Uncle John from London stayed in a hotel I was now looking forward to another holiday in the South. This time I was to visit Uncle John, Aunt Ethel cousins Elsie and Norman in Chiswick then Uncle Alf, Aunt Ciss, cousins Norman, John, Wally and Betty in Arundel Sussex then Aunt Maggie Uncle George and cousins Jim, Marjorie, George, Kitty, Joyce and Olive now living in Mitford near Godalmin. Thoughts war were not in my mind. I put my bike in the guards van and joined a crowd from work with their families and girl friends. The train left Sunderland station at 11-00pm and arrived at Kings Cross at 5-00am. I thought that it was too early to call on them so I collected my bike and toured Westminster and some other parts of London and arrived at my Uncles house at 7-30am half an hour too late to meet Norman who had set off on a camping cycling tour of Devon and Cornwall. We never did meet.

Uncle John took me on a tour of London. Buying an all day bus ticket for one shilling we visited many interesting places.

The Science Museum which displayed full scale models of dinosours, the Planetry System and Weapons of War one of which was a torpedo similar to those aimed at my ship in 1943 and 1944 then to St Dunstans Hospital for soldiers suffering from terrible wounds, blindness and amputations from the 1914-1918 war and unable to live a normal life in a home of their own. Uncle John was wounded in that war and was in a London Hospital where I believe he met and later married Ethel, not confirmed. Cousin Elsie and me went cycling to the West End taking in Richmond. Next day it was goodbye and off to Arundel to stay a couple of days with Aunt Ciss, Uncle Alf, cousins Norman, John, Wally and Betty. They lived in a cottage which was then 200 years old and it had a thatched roof.. The doors were very low and so was the ceiling in the upstairs bedroom I was to sleep in. Conversation with Uncle Alf on our first meeting was difficult. He spoke with the local accent and me with mine.

Aunt Ciss not having lost her Wearside accent understood both of us and helped us through. We soon mastered the problem.

Following the custom of country dwellers she had stocks of home made preserves and wine. While chatting with them I was given a glass of apple cider. It was lovely so I asked for a second. After that all that I can remember was going outside for some fresh air and waking up next morning in bed and bumping my head against the ceiling in the process. It must have been strong. Uncle Alf was a Cowman and game keeper on the estate of the Duke of Norfolk. He took me to the byres to see the cows being milked and in the evening went on a pigeon shoot with him and his friends. Several pigeons were bagged but I did not shoot one.

In 1914 when war broke out Aunt Ciss was already on holiday in London and she was stranded when all transport was commandeered by the miltary. Unable to get home I assume that she found work down there and met up with Alf Smart whom she married.

She lived the rest of her life in Arundel coming north to be a bridesmaid with Aunt Fran for the wedding of my Mam and Dad in 1920 and occasionally for a holiday.

I left next day for Aunt Maggie. It was dark when I reached Chichester and there were six miles of pitch black open country to cross before reaching Sidlesham. A bright beam from my bicycle lamp attracted dozens of bats. I felt the wind from them as they swished by me and I expected to struck by one at any time. On arriving at my aunts house some bats came in with me when the door was opened. The next few minutes were spent ejecting them and I was told that this happened every time that the door was opned after dark.

Next day I cycled to Portsmouth. The English Channel was so close to the road some sections were awash. I was hoping to go on board Nelsons flagship HMS Victory but it was not open to the public that day so I had to be content by viewing it from the dockside.

My holiday was coming to a close. Leaving Sidlesham I had one more night in Arundel and one more in Chiswick before returning home.

Uncle Dave was now working on a ship running the blockade to Spanish ports during the Spanish cival war

The Munich crisis in September made changes to everyday life. Many men including Doxford workmen who were in the Royal Naval Reserve or the Durham Light Infantry were called up for the emergancy. The Prime Minister Neville Chamberlain on his return from a meeting in Munich with Hitler the German Chancelor said that they had agreed peace in our time.

The crisis now over the men returned to their jobs. However in London and other cities and big towns air raid precautions (ARP) were already in force. Sunderland based its ARP headquarters in Thornholme. Warden posts (WP) and a few First Aid Posts (FAP) were set up in various parts of the town one being in the old Colliery School now closed at the Wheat Sheaf cross roads.. Posters were everywhere illustrating how to deal with different types of emergencies and ARP hints printed on cigarette cards. Deep underground shelters were installed in the public parks. Anderson air raid shelter were buried in back gardens with only the entrance exposed. In back yards brick shelters were built and where space was limited a shelter was situated beneath the dining room table. Surface shelters were installed in shipyards, engine works, factories and uother workplaces where there was space.

Just before Xmas Doreen Sampson invited us to a party to be held at her house in Givens St Roker after dancing at the Alex. We left at midnight and walking all the way passing Mowbray Park and the Public Library to the Gas Office corner in Fawcett St where the weekly maintenance work on the tramcar lines and points was in progress. The area was brightly lit up to enable the work to be carried out. Binns, Mengs restaurant and all the other shop fronts were ablaze with light enabling window shopping. We bagan the soiree with a big spread followed by games and dancing ending with breakfast at 8-00am.

Uncle Billy was engaged to Vera Murtha and they were married in St Peters Church on Boxing Day and I was their groomsman.

There was a flap when with only five minutes before the cermony was due to start Billy Woodifield the Best Man had not arrived. He showed up one minute before the bride. They set up home in Hull where he was currently working in an aircraft factory. When the war started they came home and Billy went to work in Lynns Engineering Works in Pallion.

CHAPTER 4

1939 TO 1945

1939

I spent Whit week-end with them.

Uncle Dave on learning he was to become a father he left the sea and worked as a fitter on the battleship HMS George V building in Newcastle. Early in September Aunt Fran gave birth to a baby boy and was called David.

Our way of life was soon to undergo a rapid change. The German troops invaded Poland on Friday morning 1st September. Simultaneously a German vessel a regular visitor to the Wear left with only half of its cargo of coal. The PM sent a letter of protest to Hitler with an ultimatum to withdraw his army from Poland within seventy-two hours.

It was announced over the wireless and printed in the newspapers that all lights must not be seen from outside. In other words a total black-out had been ordered. The police and air raid wardens were out that same evening enforcing the instruction. Throughout the country all night work in factories was suspended until blackout conditions had been met.

That night we all met at Professor Dorns Dancing School as usual and at the end of the session when we opened the door to leave we couldn't see our hands before us it was so dark. There were no tramway maintenance lights and the town shops which used to be ablaze with lights were now in darkness. It took awhile to accustom ourselves to the blackness and many people ended up with a black eye after colliding against a lamp-post. It became easier when the moon was shining but it also aided the bombers.

Next morning life appeared to go on as before. My young brother Bobby with his friends all about twelve years old went boating up the river as planned. On the return trip they found themselves sailing in pitch blackness. Meanwhile all their parents were anxious about their safety and the police were called in to help find them. The boys were very late when they arrived at the North Dock unaided and there found the river police waiting for them. They wondered what all of the fuss was about.

WAR DECLARED

The PM spoke to the nation over the wireless telling all that as from 11-00am today Sunday 3rd September 1939 a state of war exists between this country and Germany. As he was speaking the sirens wailed for the first time in our town sending people scurrying to air raid shelters. It was a false alarm. Following his announcement all countries within the British Empire declared war against Germany in double quick time. France was very slow to follow waiting till 6-00pm.

That Sunday morning I was playing at naval battles with my young brother Bobby using the patterned carpet for the ocean and many photos of warships of the world on cigarette cards when my Dad came upstairs and told us the news. We were war.

I was nearly eighteen but the significance of the situation did not sink in immediately and we continued with our game.

Gas masks were issued to everyone and for a short time were carried everywhere. They were cumbersome. Being lulled into a sense of false security due to an apparent lack of war inactivity it wasn`t long before people left them at home when going out.

I was already an apprentice fitter and turner at W Doxford & Son Sunderland when the war started and when I arrived at work next day I learned that all of those who had gone to the terretorial camp for two weeks training and all the other reservists would not be returning until this war was ended. Joe Lawson was already at sea see p61, 73 and homeward bound. The ship he was on was bombed and strafed when nearing a north-east port. As a result Joe suffered badly from nerves and was discharged and started work as a fitter on permanent night shift at Doxford. I did not know him but when I went on twelve hour shifts day and night alternatively I met him in the canteen one night in the summer of 1941.

The town was closed for three weeks. The army installed check points on every road at the town boundaries and no one was allowed in or out of town without official permission. Public entertainment suffered. The Roker Park football ground, roller skating at the Rink, dance halls, cinemas and theatres were all closed presumably in the interest of crowd safety. When the restrictions were eased national football was changed to regional and most other entertainments were re-instated. Roller skating remained banned till after the end of the war. As a result ballroom dancing instead of being seasonal carried on all year.

During the last months of 1939 thousands of children living in industrial areas all over the country were evacuated to so called safe places. I accompanied my brother to the Central Railway Station where he was to join others from his school. The train pulled away leaving many mothers in tears, my Mam couldn`t face a parting at the station. His group was bound for Langtoft a small village in North Yorkshire a few miles from Driffield aerodrome a prime military target. His first billet was Mr Ogden the village schoolmaster. He wasn`t happy there and was moved to live at the home of Mrs Simpson

One Sunday Mam, Dad and me paid them a visit and we were were favourably impressed by her. He was quite happy but when school friends started to return to their homes it wasn`t long before he was back.

As soon as I was turned eighteen I was put on the two shift system 6-00am till 2-00pm and 2-00pm til 10-00pm each with a half hour break. Not having the time to ride home for my break I used the bus, the fare was a penny-halfpenny return.

At 5-00m workmen began boarding the bus at the Fulwell Depot and 5-30am at the Wheat Sheaf I and other passengers would get on board where the men were smoking cigarettes making the air thick with blue smoke, they were coughing and spluttering and it was worse on the upper deck. One reason why I did not take up smoking.

A few days after war was declared I volunteered to be a messenger boy at the Colliery School FAP. Only three full time staff were employed there. Ted Steel in his sixties and two young women Peggy Potts and Winnie Bousefield. There were about a dozen middle aged volunteers. I fully expected to practice delivering messages between the various posts but the only messages I done was to go to the shops for cigarettes. I was learning nothing so I gave it up.

1940

Rationing was introduced on 8 January 1940 which for one person was 4oz of butter and 4oz of bacon per week. As time went on the following items were added. Meat, margarine,sweets, cooking fats, clothing, paper and petrol. This went on until the 1950s when the last item was finally removed from the ration book.

Static water tanks were installed in many streets in readiness for the eventuality of any water supplies being cut in an air raid.

Easter Monday I along with others of my age group went to the Labour Exchange in Tatham St to register for conscription into the armed services. I volunteered for the Royal Navy. From the eighteen Doxford apprentices who registered twelve received their call-up papers by the week-end. I was not one of them.

Double summer time was introduced which meant that it remained light until after 11-00pm for several weeks. 11-00pm was the time that the air raid siren often went off once the raids began in earnest. For several months all was quiet on the Home Front and in France. At home it did not appear that we were at war except for the steady increase of men and women in uniform to be seen in uniform and the French sailors who came dancing at the New Rink. This period was known as the Phoney War but off the coast our convoys were being bombed daily. When the sirens were sounded in the early days of the war most people went in the nearest public air raid shelter and workers in the works shelter.

In mid-winter it was so cold on some days that machines were unable to start up until braziers burning coke were brought in to warm them up.

THE FIRST AIR RAID ON SUNDERLAND

When the fishermens cottages at Whitburn were bombed on the 2nd June people from all over town including me flocked to see the damaged houses and the bomb crators in the field close by. Very soon we would not have to travel far to see bomb damage. For many it would be in their own street.

On the afternoon of 5 August when I was at work the sirens sounded and we all made for the surface shelters. Standing at the entrance I had a good view of the air battle taking place over Fulwell across the river. Several Junkers 88 dropped their bombs on the streets of houses below throwing up clouds of smoke and dust.

RAF planes from Usworth airfield nearby tore into them and at least one enemy plane was shot down and none of ours.

Five cottages in Annie St received direct hits and were totally demolshed. One was next door to Aunt Frans cottage. She was covered in soot and dust when the ceilings came down but she escaped unhurt. Returning from work Uncle Dave was shocked on entering his street and saw the state of his home.

Shortly after this incident he left his shore job and rejoined the Merchant Navy and crossed the North Atlantic many times and came out of the war unscathed but died from an illness in 1952.

About noon Friday 9 August a lone raider swept in from the sea and dropped bombs on a ship. It slewed across the river before settling on the bottom preventing other ships from entering or leaving the port for a few days. My Mam was crossing the Wearmouth Bridge it then dropped a bomb on the railway bridge over the street next to the bridge. The plane then followed the river up to Laings shipyard and dropped a bomb killing four workmen and wounding others. It flew away unapposed then the sirens were sounded.

The bombing of the fishermens cottages, Fulwell, the sunken ship, the railway bridge and the strafing of the foot bridge and Laings shipyard made people realise that there really was a war on prompting many to join one of the various sections of the ARP.

After these incidents I volunteered again but this time as a first aider at the Colliery School First Aid Post. FAP.

A lot of young boys and girls as well as married couple signed on this Post. The ARP was reorganised resulting in Winnie Bousefield and Peggy Potts being transferred to Thornholme regional headquarters. Ted Steel well over sixty remained as storekeeper. After a few months there was about one hundred volunteers on this Post. They came from all walks of life. Shipyards, engine works, shops, factories, coal miners, solicitors and doctors. Alf Madden and Jack Snowdon were members of the St Johns Ambulance Brigade and they organised first aid parties and practice sessions. When these parties were formed I was only eighteen and my only qualification in first aid was gained when I was a member of Whitburn St Chapel Boys Brigade. After several weeks practicing I was made a member of a party of four men and a nurse. The parties were put on a rota, drivers were put on a different rota. After an alert was sounded the first driver and party members to arrive formed a scratch party in case of a quick call out. As the people for duty arrived they would take over and the others would fall out. It was a simple and workable scheme. When a night alert was long and quiet a party not on standby would unofficially go out on the streets and visit the various local air raid shelters mainly to get the people singing to help lift their spirits. George Gray a friend from work happened to be in one that we visited and he sang "The Miners Dream Of Home" and others followed his example.

In January on the coldest day this winter chaos reigned. Walking home from workI saw tramcars, their wheels frozen to the rails in Southwick Rd.and motor cars unable to plough the deep snow coming to a halt. All over town trams, cars and lorries were abandoned, the drivers and passengers forced to walk to their destinations.

At the First Aid Post one night shortly after the evacuation from Dunkirk and other French ports we heard over the wireless Winston Churchills stirring speech about blood, tears, toil and sweat.

He made us feel that we could repel all invaders with broomsticks.

A number of Wearmouth Miners were volunteers and they tried to persuade me to leave Doxford and work as a fitter with them in the mine. I told them that I wouldn`t go down the pit for all the tea in China. By 1968 I had worked in several industries turning out totally different products so for another change I went to Vane Tempest and Seaham for training and for the rest of my working life worked at Wearmouth Colliery retiring in 1982. I received no tea.

It wasn`t all bandaging in the FAP, we made into a social gathering as well. Soon we had a small billiard table, a dart board, a table tennis, a gramophone and records which when played some of us danced to the music. This gave birth to the idea of having social evenings. As an experiment one was organised for a Saturday evening. It was a huge success and it became a weekly event even during the quiet alerts. When a piano was aquired John Punshen offered to play it for us on the social evenings.

One September night I had just retired to bed when I heard the sirens. In less than ten minutes I was dressed and on my way to the FAP. For a long time all was quiet and I stood in the yard watching hundreds of shooting stars. Suddenly the searchlights came on and stabbed the night sky near Whitburn searching for the intruder. An enemy plane was caught in a cluster of lights and it was then passed from one battery to another until it was almost directly overhead.

All this time the ack-ack guns were firing away and it was surrounded by puffs of smoke from the bursting shells and then it received a direct hit on the fuselage and it hurtled to earth. The wreckage and the bodies of the crew were scattered over a large area and in Ward St Hendon a woman was killed when part of the wreckage fell on her.

One of the volunteers Abert Beatty was a lay preacher and on a Sunday evening he hosted a prayer meeting in the FAP. Regardless of their religous beliefs almost everyone attended his meetings.

We were issued with uniforms consisting of a beret, battle blouse, overcoat, trousers and a pair of boots, we already had a gas mask and steel helmet.

One day at work I heard a rumour that the Germans had attempted an invasion on the Northumberland coast but were repelled by burning oil on the sea.

Another rumour was that the skin from concentration camp victims was used to make shades for table lamps. These rumours persisted but to my knowledge were never confirmed by the media or officially.

By the start of the year so many men had been called to the colours there was now an acute shortage of skilled workers in the heavy industries. To redress this problem the government intrduced The Essential Works Order. This meant that while this act was in force no one could change their job unless under special circumstances.

Because the coal mines were severely undermanned many men now being called up for the forces were sent to the mines instead. They were called Bevin Boys named after the minister who had dreamed up the scheme.

Hundreds of miners already in the forces were released and returned to their former collieries. One of them was Tommy Watson who on returning home and to Wearmouth Colliery came to our Post as a volunteer. We met and struck up a friendship and became lifelong friends. Tommy and me went all over together, first aid duties, cinema, walking, dancing at the FAP, TA drill hall in Dykelands Rd, Seaburn Hall, Bay Hotel, St Benet church hall, St mark church hall, Swan St School,

Jeffrey Hall, Binns recreation hall. Now and again we went to the Oxford Galleries and the Milvern in Newcastle. Once we went to the Durham Ice Rink. For me it was a disaster. After a few circuits I nose dived into a wide stretch of water and I was soaked through. I vowed then no more ice skating for me. Forty years on I went ice skating twice a week for ten years at Crowtree Leisure Centre without mishap except in the first two weeks I was twice pulled down

Alf Graham see p18, 43 joined Colliery FAP as a first aider. One day when in conversation with him it came out that it was him who had been resposible for the thumps that I had heard all those years ago. As a new tenant he had moved into the empty flat next door to ours. Some nights after closing time he left the pub, go home and climb up the stairs. He had only one natural leg, the other was a wooden one and it was this that made the thump. The thumps stopped when he carpeted the stairs.

Hendie Ellison a drummer in Jack Lillies dance band joined this Post and when he learned about our social evenings he joined in and played the drum alongside John Punshen. H e then persuaded Jack Lillie and Norman Snowdon who like him were miners at Wearmouth Pit to join the post. With them and John Punshen we ended up with a four piecedance band who played at our socials when they were not engaged to play elsewhere.

A few weeks later Norman Snowdon left the pit for health reasons and came to work at Doxford in the same machine shop as me.

On the 7th November the Post was full with one party on standby, the rest were playing darts, billiards, table tennis or just sitting around. It was ten-o-clock normal closing time for pubs. About twenty minutes later I was outside in the yard watching the shooting stars. I heard a plane coming toward me from the sea and up Roker Avenue then the bomb came screaming down. It hit the Blue Bell pub about 300yards away. Being so close to the incident the standby party without waiting for orders from Thornholme dashed to the scene. Meanwhile the warden had evidently reported no casualties therefore Thornholme had no reason to contact us. An hour later the alert was still on and our party was still at the bombed pub. Another party was sent along to investigate. No one thought of contacting Thornholme. On their arrival groans were heard and expecting the worst went into the cellar and there found the missing party sitting down with empty and full bottles scattered around them oblivious to the war or anything else.

In another alert no bombs were dropped near us that night but we had one casualty. A sailor walked into our Post with a piece of shrapnel embedded in his hand and asked for help. He had only just arrived back in England after the naval battle of Matapan in March and was on his way home for some leave. An alert was on but all was quiet when he arrived at the railway station.

It was after ten-o-clock and the trams and buses had stopped running for the night so he had no alternative but to walk. As he turned into Fulwell Rd from Roker Avenue enemy planes flew overhead on a bombing raid to another area and were met by heavy ack-ack fire and he was hit on the hand by a falling piece of shrapnel.

To keep production going a scheme was devised whereby when a general alert was sounded Fire Watchers in the works would give the alarm if there was imminent danger. In a general alert of several hours the works siren was notsounded until danger was imminent proving the system to be good for production.

On night on the 12 hour night shift I went home at nine for my one hour break Returning to work I was passing the Southwick Green when bombs fell on the Cato St area. The blast blew me off my bike leaving me shaken and dusty but not much hurt. A few minutes later the warning siren was sounded. When I arrived at Doxford I went to the ambulance room for a check up. The nurse gave me a sedative then I cleaned myself up and off to my lathe. The men were back at work after being in the shelter. Soon after this the all clear was sounded.

1941

There was a very bad raid on the 5th April from 10-15pm. A land mine was dropped near to the Victoria Hall completely destroying it and much of the surrounding streets. No more dancing there for us. We had been there the previous night and the bandsmen having an engagement to play again in two days time had left their instruments in the hall. Also destroyed were the tropical plants and parrots in the Mowbray Park Winter Gardens. The goldfish were blown from the inside pool into the lake outside, some of them lived on for many years.

We began our search for survivors in the demolished Empress Hotel in Union St. and after three hours I found that I had crossed over a large devastated area ending up in Tathem St. The all clear sounded at 5-00am just in time for me to go work

1942

Grandma Blenkinsop suffered a stroke and died at home in Rothsay St in February and was buried in Mere Knoll Cemetery. Two of my workmates George Kerr, George Moore, Uncle Vin and myself were her poll bearers.

Fire Watchers were men and women not already in any of the services were now compelled to do fire watching at their place of work. I believe they had to do at least one duty each week.

There were many alerts this year but people got used to them and carried on with their business and leisure only making for shelter when things got a bit too hot. Many of these alerts were without incidents. Most of the raiders dropped their bombs over a wide area resulting in many houses being destroyed and causing several casualties each time

The manager of the Laburnum Cottage pub had a daughter and she was twenty-one years old. Tommy Watson, a few from the Post and myself were invited to her coming of age party. It was held on a Sunday evening and on arrival and in spite of rationing we were set down to a lovely spread.

Party games and dancing went on till midnight then we all left for home. We were almost in the town when we heard the sirens. We quickened our pace and made our way to our FAP. At 1-00am a land mine was dropped behind the Laburnum Cottage pub demolishing several streets and there many casualties. The pub was damaged but no one in it was hurt. Our FAP was not involved

Periodically full scale exercises took place in various parts of the town on a Sunday morning. On the 1st May an exercise was held on the new fire station in Station Rd. Fulwell and lasted more than six hours. In the exercise I was a casualty and I lay down on the flat roof where I was supposed to have been blown by the bomb blast. A first aid party came to my rescue, bandaged me up, strapped me to a stretcher and gently lowered me to the ground. Other casualties in and around the fire station were attended to. Our roles were then reversed and I became a rescuer and first aider.

That very same night Fulwell was raided and bombs damaged the fire station and the nearby Fulwell Workmans Club. In a raid some weeks later Symerna House where we sometimes practiced was totally destroyed.

Sea Rd School Fulwell was taken over as a First Aid Post and many volunteers were transferred from the Colliery FAP to Sea Rd FAP it being more convenient. They continued coming to our weekly socials but after a short while they organised there own. From then on a social was held in each Post on alternative Saturdays.

I danced and flirted with most of the girls at both Posts and at other halls but I had no thoughts of marriage in the middle of a war nor had Tommy.

While attending night classes in the Technical College Green Terrace I made friends with Norman Gray and Derek Alderson see p102. They were Rover Scouts and I often went with them to St Gabriels Church and took part in some of their activities.

Some nights after class we went to the YMCA in Toward Rd where we played table tennis and badminton with Jeanette McDonald, Mary Rufus and others.

Easter week-end I went with their troop and camped on a farmers field on one bank of the River Coquet near Felton. On a hilltop nearby was a church. One night after dark we went up to this church

The doors were not locked and we dared each other to go down the aisle to the alter. I was still a little bit superstitious and the atmosphere was scary and creepy and we were at first afraid to venture inside. The fear of the unknown was overcome and one by one we all accepted the challenge.

Next day we tied a rope to a tree on each river bank and took turns hauling ourselves across getting a ducking in the process. Tree climbing was another activity. I was lopping off tree branches and twigs for the camp fire. While chopping sticks the axe gashed my left fore finger and I was taken to the local surgery to have it stitched. It left a permanent scar

Going to the farmhouse to buy eggs and milk I noticed that their clock was two hours behind ours. The farmer told me that he didn`t observe national clock time nor did the cows, they had to be milked every day at the same time.

A coal fire was used for cooking and heating. Paraffin oil lamps for illumination, gas and electricity was not available.

A few weeks later some of the lads were called up and one of them did not survive the war.

In the summer aiming to have a rest from the regular air raid alerts I went with my workmates Willie Carnagie, Jimmy Aylen on a cycling and camping holiday for a week in the Lake District. The tents and kitbags holding the rest of the gear was sent on ahead by train so that we had no baggage to carry on our bikes. We met and left the town on Sunday at 7-00am and facing a strong headwind we pushed and puffed our way to Barnard Castle and there rested for a little while. We arrived in Keswick about nine-o-clock and went to the station to collect our equipment only to learn that the station was closed on Sundays. We went back up the road to the Fitz Park and looked around for a wam place to kip. Right opposite to the park a woman looking from her window had seen us arrive and go to the station and back. Guessing our plight she came over and told us that she took in boarders and offered us a room for the night at a cheap rate.

After breakfast we went to the railway station to collect the tents and other gear. We searched around to find a site on which to pitch the tents.

Every day was fine and warm and we cycled round most of the lakes. I climbed Latrigg my first mountain then Helvelyn my second. In the years to come I will climb most of the mountains in the Lake District.

One night raiders passed overhead on their way to Merseyside and we were disturbed by the sirens. We came here so as not to hear them. Back home they were silent all the while that we were away.

Now back home from holiday and back at work I was put on the 6-00am till 2-00pm for seven days. On the following week Mondays, Wednesdays, Fridays 2-00pm till 6-00am Tuesdays and Thursdays 2-00pm till 10-00pm until further notice.

As a matter of interest Willie Carnagie became a professor at Birmingham University and two or three years later Jimmy Aylen went to sea and in 1946 he became ill and died in hospital in Buenos Aires Argentina. I was there in 1947 and after my ship had sailed homeward bound my Argentinean friends that I had made went back to the cemetery and took photographs of his grave and sent them on to me. I did not have a camera. When I returned home I called on his mother and widow and gave them photos of his grave.

1943

Sunderland suffered its worst air raids in March, April and May of this year.

The March air raid was concentrated on the town centre. St Thomas Church was totally destroyed some of the debris landing in my back yard on the other side of the river. The three large department stores of Binns were badly damaged by incendiary bombs. One was in John St and two were in Fawcett St To enable trading to continue Binns rented several small shops around the town centre.

The April air raid. A week later the raiders came again and dropped incendiary bombs on the town centre. Strange as it may seem most of the shops rented out to Binns were hit and set on fire while the adjacent building escaped serious damage.

THAT AWFUL NIGHT IN MAY

The third began on a Saturday evening in May and I think that it was the worst and heaviest raid of all and it was concentrated on Monkwearmouth but bombs fell on many other parts of town including Sunderland Roker Park football ground.

The build up to that awful night in May began about eight nights earlier when alerts lasting nearly all night and every night without incidents. I was at work so unable to report for duty. On the Friday I began work at 2-00pm and worked through till 6-00am. Instead of going to bed which I normally do I washed and changed. I then had breakfast and went to meet my FAP friend George Buckley and went to Garnsworthys gaage in Rutland St Millfield and picked up a lorry loaded with empty milk churns. They were to be delivered to a farm in Cowgate. It was early evening when we got back to the garage just in time to go home and change for the dance which was to be held in Swan St School. Three dances later the sirens sounded the warning.and we all dashed to the Post. Within fifteen minutes the Post was ready for action. Ater three hours of inactivity the party that I was in and not on standby went out and visited the local public air shelters. This was a regular routine when sufficient volunteers were on hand.

This night we called at the shelter in Bonners Field below the Bromarsh cinema which was built on stilts and level with the Wearmouth Bridge. We found it empty except for a couple of men waiting to tell us that everyone was tired of spending the previous six nights out of bed with nothing happening. Leaving the empty shelter we returned to the Post. An hour later the planes came and heavily bombed the area. People must have returned to the shelter when the bombs rained down because one party was sent to the shelter in Bonners field which had received a direct hit and casualties were expected. The Bromarsh had disappeared. The party I was with was sent to Waterloo St at the bottom of Bonners Field near the Ferryboat Landing.

What devastation, whole streets had collapsed. Many room lights were shining. We did not put them out as they helped us while attending to the casualties. They could have aided the bombers but as fires were burning all around I don`t think that it mattered. The local baths were used as a morgue.

I had never before or since seen so many dead peope. The injured were taken away in ambulances. A rescue party had been called in from South Shields to help. Later I was told by one of them that a man trapped by a beam holding up a wall volunteered to stay put while rescuers crawled beneath him and dragged people out. When he was pulled clear the wall collapsed. After the all clear we continued with our efforts and it was mid-afternoon when it was decided that no more survivors would be found so we went home. I washed, had tea then lay down for an hour before going to the Post service followed by a few games of table tennis. I went home and went to bed hoping to have a good sleep. At 1-00am the sirens disturbed my slumber and I was off to the First Aid Post again and I stayed until 5-00am when I had to leave to start work at 6-00am. After an hour the all clear was given. There were no incidents. At the end of my shift I dashed home, had tea then off to night school followed by a couple of hours dancing at the New Rink.

Going to bed I wondered when I was going to have a good night sleep. I enjoyed one that very night followed by many more. I was never disturbed by the sirens again. The Luftwaffa had visited Sunderland for the last time.

After this raid 64 rocket guns were sited at Seaburn and many oil burners ready to make smoke screens were placed all around the perimeter of the town. These were in addition to our regular defences of ack-ack guns and barrage balloons. It paid off because although there were still raids on the North-East Coast they avoided Sunderland.

From my notes there more than 200 alerts each one lasting anything up to eight hours. Bombs were dropped during 42 of them and at least two without a warning.

267 people died, about a thousand injured. one third of them seriously

The Sunderland Star Newspaper printed 3 April 1995 reported the following

Sunderland suffered 250 alerts, 22 bombing raids dropping 385 HE, 32 parachute mines, 36 firepots, 23 phosphorous. Worst raid was on 24 May 1943. 267 people died, more than 700 injured, more than 1,000 houses destroyed, 34,500 houses damaged,

John Buckley FAP, Army. Believed killed in Germany

Howard Crooks FAP, RAF. Died when his plane was shot down over Germany

George Bell FAP, MN Looking back I sometimes wonder how I and thousands more like me were able to cope under such strenuous times. My worst and most frightening experience in six years of war was during the last air raid on the town

When the air raids on the town appeared to have ended my thoughts turned to my earlier ambition "To go to sea". Joe Lawson see p49, 73 a man I was to meet and become friends with. He was already on the Shipping Pool and was an engineer on a ship when the war started and was homeward bound when the ship was bombed and strafed. Suffering from nerves he was invalided from the MN and started work on permanent nightshift at Doxford Engine Works.

Once again my shift times were changed to seven days starting at 6-00am till 6-00pm then five nights starting 6-00pm till 6-00am. I was able to cycle home for the 9-00pm break but for the 3-00am break I went to the canteen and it was there that I met Joe Lawson.

MV EMPIRE HOUSMAN

Early in June while working at my lathe a stranger aproached me and introduced himself as Mr Gilbert chief engineer of a vessel being built and engined here at Doxfords. He then told me that Joe Lawson see p , p , p ,was going to join this ship when it was ready for sea and he had mentioned the fact that I was interested in going to sea. When I had satisfied him that was true he offered me a berth on condition that I could secure my release from the Essential Works Order. Billy Francis another workmate on the oposite shift to me was also offered a berth under the same conditions.

Every fortnight for the next five months when on night shift I travelled to the Shipping Office on the Newcastle Quay-side trying to secure my release. It was early November when they fainally agreed to release us.

We were the last two men from Doxfords to be released until after the Essential Works Order terminated at the end of the war. Meanwhile when I was on day shift I used the Canteen on a day when ENSA staged a show. One of them was Frank Formby who performed a similar routine as his brother George with his ukulele.

One day on my way to the Canteen for dinner and to see the show I met the Second Mate of the ship being fitted out at the quay and I introduced myself to him and explained that with a bit of luck I could be sailing with him. I had a few more weeks to wait before I was released.

I visited my Southern relatives again this summer calling on Uncle John in 72 Silver Crescent Chiswick. While there I visited the Covent Garden Opera

House where a band played dance music. After a few tunes the stage revolved to bring Ivy Benson and her all girl band into the limelight. These two bands took turns at playing all evening. I danced with a girl from Tottenham who thought that I was a foreigner. I told her that I was Norwegian and she said that I spoke good English. I wonder who was kidding who? I then had a couple of days with Aunt Ciss, Uncle Alf and cousins in Arundel. I then visited Aunt Maggie, Uncle George and cousins now living in Mitford near Guildford. While there I saw wave after wave of RAF planes passing overhead. They were probably taking part in one of the many thousand bomber raids now being inflicted on Germany.

I bade goodbye to my friends in the Colliery First Aid Post and the Sea Rd. Post where I had spent three happy years but going out on incidents were in some cases traumatic, revolting, bloodcurdling and to say quite simply horrible.

After eight years working for Doxfords I put my notice in to enable me to enter the Merchant Navy. My last shift ended at 6-00am Saturday 2nd December 1943.

For the last few months I had been on piece work eighty hours a week and my biggest pay before offtakes was £5-2s-6d.

On Monday 4th Dec Joe Lawson, Billy Francis and me went to the Shipping Office in Tatham St to sign Articles A on the MV Empire Housman. I was now in the Merchant Navy and the salary was £17-00 per month plus £10-00 danger money. The total being £27-00s-00d per month.

By this time I had given more than ten pints of blood to the Blood Transfusion Service enough for me to be awarded a blood donors badge. If I had remained at Doxfords I would have continued giving blood and perhaps become eligble for a silver badge.

AN EXTRACT FROM ARTICLES A

1   The voyage to terminate after two years or when the vessel docks in a United Kingdom Port whichever is the soonest.
2   Day work in the U.K. 9-00am till 4-00pm
3   Day work in a foreign port or at sea 7-00am till 4-30pm
4   Watches at sea fours on and eight hours off every day.
5   Manouvering in ports, rivers and canals. Two hour standby duties before and after watch.
6   Work MUST be carried out between watches at the discretion of the 2nd engineer

Monday at 9-00am Billy and me returned to Doxfords as Merhant Navy Engineer Officers wearing white overalls. We walked proudly among our former workmates chatting with them in passing.

Our main duties wereto observe the main engines in the various stages of construction in the Erecting Shop and on the MV Empire Housman fitting out at the quay. It was the prototype of a new design. Solid bulkheads now separate the holds from each other. There is now no watertight door between the engine room and the tunnel. Access to the tunnel will be on ladders from the accommodation amidship and from the steering flat aft. It was claimed that it will be difficult to sink her.

Until the accommodation was ready for use we went home every day at 4-00pm

The old police station in West Wear St had been converted into a Royal Naval gunnery training school and we were instructed on how to strip Bofus and Oerlikon anti-aircraft guns and how to assemble ammunition magazines. We practised simulation shooting against aircraft on a screen. Similar to computer games of the 1970s.

Our education continued next day on the Whitburn rifle range. A model plane about six feet above the ground was hauled along guide rails by wires. At a range of about 100yds we were asked to shoot at it. When it was my turn I aimed and when it was in my sights I pulled the trigger. The tail dropped off.. The instructor was not pleased. I must take after my Dad, he was an excellant shot.

In the last war and among other things he was a sniper. Our next excersise was the firing of a rocket gun. This was a circular steel chamber with four rocket guides welded on opposite sides. I went inside the chamber and clashed the door beind me. Unknown to me the firing mechanism was very sensitive and when the door clashed the rockets soared skywards fortunately toward the sea. I sat down and took aim then pressed the firing button. All that I could see was the target bouy bobbing up and down on the water. Someone banged on the door for me to come out. Rocket drill came to a halt. At the end of the session we all came away with a certificate for completing the course. The ship was manned with fully trained army and navy gunners. They were known as Defence Equipped Merchant Ships DEMS. and we were only expected to take over as a last resort.

I was allocated to the portside Oerlickon on the boat deck. The powers that be must have been in a desparate hurry to get the ship away before Xmas. There was still a lot of work to be done before it would be ready to carry cargoes. The Empire Housman was to be completed in New York

Then came the day. Tugboats towed us down the river and just as we were approaching the Wearmouth Bridge I came up on deck and I saw a crowd of people waving down to us as we passed beneath. We drydocked at Greenwells where the hull was to be red leaded and all the valves for the hull below the waterline were to fitted. Another day over and it was time to go home again. I was enjoying this new life style, a seven hour day, two hours for lunch and only five days a week.

I hadn`t yet experienced the drawbacks of maritime life but I was to be initiated into the realities of sea life next day. It was a Friday with the week-end off to look forward to. The ship was floated out of the dock and tied up at the quay.

Stores were arriving alongside and all hands were drafted to bring them on board. Just before 4-00pm the Second Engineer told me to go below and help to prepare for sea. It came as a shock as I had no inkling that we were anywhere near ready for a sea voyage. I hadn`t realised that the ship was still full of workmen and would not be going to sea. I had a lot to learn. I informed him that all of my gear was still at home and he told me to go and collect it but hurry as we were due to sail in an hour. He didn`t say that we were just goung to another berth. I soon learned that he was the type of man who pulled rank. Time was to prove that he was an unpopular man on the ship. I dashed home, collected my things, said "ta-ra" to Mam and Dad and hurried away arriving with just a few minutes to spare.

We moved slowly away from the quayside, my thoughts well and truly mixed up. Here I was sailing into the unknown leaving behind friends I had intended to be with that evening. I was operating the telegraph and about fifteen minutes later it rang the signal "Finished with engines" I couldn`t believe it. When I went on deck I saw that we were still in the river tied to a buoy. There was no shore leave. During the next two days the ship went through the sea trials. After successfuly completing the measured mile between Sunderland and Cullercoats we returned to the two Roker breakwaters where a pilot cutter was waiting to take the pilot and workmen from the ship. We sailed to South Shields and picked up a river pilot who guided us upriver to Hebburn where we were to have torpedo nets fitted. De-gausing gear meant to repel mines was also to be fitted. Next day we sailed down river to South Shields and there the river pilot left us. Loaded only with about two thousand tons of coke as ballast we sailed outward bound for New York where the unfinished work was to be completed. We sailed steadily north along the north-east coast of England and the east coast of Scotland then entered the Pentland Firth. The waters here were very stormy and the ship was pitching and tossing like a bucking bronco. Once through we turned south and finally entered the calm waters of Loch Ewe in the early hours of Xmas Eve. It was a Royal Naval Base where convoys were formed to go to America, Africa and the Middle East.

Merchant ships were arriving all day and by nightfall there were at least one hundred merchant ships in addition to aircraft carriers, cruisers, destroyers, frigates, corvettes and sloops of the Royal Navy.

Listening to the news on the wireless we heard that the German pocket battleship had just been sunk and as their submarine wolf packs had recently suffered huge losses.

It looked as though we could expect a reasonable quiet voyage with only the weather to contend with.

At dusk the ships began to move slowly from their moorings and left the Loch to take up their position in the convoy that was being formed. I was off duty so I stayed on deck to watch the flotilla. We moved out at 9-00pm.

A sea watch is of four hours but when manouvering the watch begins two hours before, the reason being there is a lot of auxilliary machinery in use which is normally idle when at sea. My normal watch starts at midnight but tonight I went on at 10-00pm. At 4-00am standby was still in operation so I stayed in the engine room till 6-00am. I showered then took to my bunk.

At 11-am I went on deck and saw row upon row of ships stretching to the horizons. It was an unforgettable sight. We were now passing the north coast of Ireland and the sea was very rough and as time passed it became stormier and our speed was reduced to two knots. This was to keep the propeller under water. At a higher speed it would rise above the waves and revolve faster causing damage to the main engine. Most of the other vessels and crewmen would be suffering the same discomfort. According to the experienced seamen this was the worst storm they had encountered. I learned that the best place to be under these conditions was on the middle of the engine room floor. Only at this point was there no rolling felt but plenty of pitching. Unfortunately to be there one had to be on watch.

After three days the heavy seas eased off a lot but it was still rough and when daylight came we saw that of the hundred or more ships in the convoy there was now a group of eight ships. They formed a line ahead, our ship in seventh place.

The short line of ships pressed on at the highest possible speed hoping to catch up with the main convoy in the next couple of days. We were now appproaching the wide expanse of ocean not patrolled by allied warships. They were unable to carry sufficient fuel to cover that area. The Happy Hunting Grounds was the phrase given by the German submarine commanders.

The weather continued to be atrocious and was now snowing hard and mountainous waves breaking over the bow. The seamen had their work cut out chipping the ice from the deck and the rigging and shovelling as much snow as possible overboard to keep the top weight down.

One morning the second engineer who was on watch hauled me out of bed to do work in addition to my watch. I complained but he reminded me that according to Articles A that I had signed I had no choice but to go with him.. I went with him to the stern where the stern gland was in need of packing.

Not being seaworthy this and lots of other jobs ought to have been done before sailing.from Doxfords. When it was completed I just had time to get a bite to eat before my watch.

ENEMY ACTION

My main duties when going on watch were to go down into the tunnel to inspect all the shaft bearings and ensure that they were not overheating, enter the engine room go down three platforms and at each log the temperatures of oil, fresh and sea water.

Operate the various pumps when needed. On standby to answer the telegraph.

Once again Articles A was to be enforced. One morning after only a couple of hours sleep I was roused and told to inspect all the winches to make sure that all were in working order.

The weather is no better, it is snowing heavily and the ship is pitching and rolling..

In the evening around 8-00pm I was in the saloon with some of the other off duty officers when we heard the alarm bells ringing.

The lookout reported that a torpedo had passed across our bow. This incident prompted our Skipper to order both torpedo nets to be slung into position at first light.

Many years later while in the Sunderland library I was reading "The Chronology of the war at sea" by J Rowher. I learned that it was Lt.CommanderCount Keller U731 who had attempted to torpedo our Ship.

The following night at one bell which was fifteen minutes before midnight my steward as always came into my room with a cup of tea and woke me. Time to go on watch. I hurried to the after deck, inspected the steering gear then down into the tunnel to inspect the bearings. The memory of the torpedo miss urged me not to loiter. After quickly feeling the casing of each bearing I was up the ladder in double quick time p and into the accommodation. Going along the corridor I stopped at the engine room door. It was about midnight ships time and into New Years Eve 31st December 1943 when I pushed the door open and stepped on to the engine room top grating I heard a very loud bang. The ship shuddered and the main engine stopped instantly. I didn`t know it at the time but a torpedo had blown the rudder and propeller away flooding the after hold. Some of the seamen sleeping above the steering flat suffered only minor bruises. The watch keeper on the bridge heard the explosion and panicked. He dashed to the boat deck and single handed tried to lower a lifeboat resulting in its side being stove in. This was the start of seventy two hours of vigil and work by all members of the crew in an atempt to keep the vessel afloat.

The engineers were changing watches and when I looked down I saw them both struggling at the controls. Because of the engine room noises they would not have heard the explosion so I slid down the ladders meaning to tell them what I thought had happened. With a crisis on their hands they were in no mood to bother with a junior engineer so I left them to it. Then I saw water spurting from the empty rivet holes, another job for New York. By now they had calmed down and I showed them the water pouring through the rivet holes and told them that I thought that we had been hit. They set the pumps away and then decided to call the bridge to find out what was happening. There was no reply. Later when the Captain came into the engine room we thought it was in response to our call.

He was shown the flowing waters and that was the first he knew of what was going on. When it was clear that the ship was not sinking we set about bunging the holes up with wood. Apart from the main engine all the other machinery was in working order.

By morning we all knew the true situation and steps were taken to go to every bulkhead to plug the empty rivet holes.

Transferring oil and water from the after tanks to those forward kept the bow down and the stern up. The large hole in the ship was now above water level and the sea was only coming in on the rise and fall of the ship and the pumps kept the level of water in the hold under control.

The third engineer tried to start the lifeboat engine. It was frozen solid. I helped him to remove it from the bedplate and took it into the engine room then stripped it down to enable the parts to thaw.

Additional portable pumps were brought into service and they were flogged mercilessly and I spent a lot of my time on the lathe turning out spare parts.

A pre-arranged plan had been devised in the event of having to take to the boats. The plan was that in daylight the motorised lifeboat was to attempt to round up the other boats and link them together. Meanwhile the wireless operator had already sent out a Mayday distress signal. At the break of dawn an aircraft from a RAF base in Iceland found us.

1944

We had air cover all day and when it turned dark another plane took over. It swept the sea with a searchlight keeping any enemy submarines submerged. On the third day about 3-00pm just before it turned dark the pilot by using an Aldis lamp told us that a destroyer was on its way and it would reach us within the hour and he was returning to base leaving us all alone. On hearing this news I packed my cases and got dressed in my best clothes and awaited the arrival of the destroyer. The scene was that of a crowd of people standingby their luggage waiting for the coach to take them away on holiday. We waited all evening for the rescue ship but it did not arrive.

It is time for me to go on watch on the start of 3rd January 1944 and I was dead beat and after having performed the usual checks the senior watch keeper told me to sit down and rest. A few minutes later he was shaking me and telling me that we had been hit again. A message from the bridge told us to come up topside. From the engine room I crossed the corridor to my room where I collected my life jacket and overcoat.

The moon was shining and it was snowing. Some ratings and the Second Mate were already at the lifeboat station on the boat deck when I arrived. A few minutes later another torpedo hit us. When a third torpedo struck the ship the order to abandon ship was given. The lifeboat was lowered and in single file the men clambered over the gunwale and down the Jacob ladder into the boat. When the last man was over the side I was told to go. Halfway down I looked up and saw the Second Mate astride the gunwale and at that instant a fourth torpedo passed beneath our lifeboat and into the side of the ship. The explosion pushed the lifeboat away from the ship and I was left clinging to the ladder as the ship rolled one way then the other. When it settled I dropped into the water and my wrist watch was stopped at 01-15am

THE RESCUE

I saw several red lights bobbing up and down on the water. A lifeboat went round picking the sailors up. Because of floating wreckage and the tangled torpedo net which had prevented the earlier torpedo from entering the engine room.

About fifteen minutes went by before I was hauled into the lifeboat.

The water wasn't too cold because we were in the Gulf Stream. This was fortunate for me and the others who had to take to the waters. On the after deck were several men. Because of the wreckage we could not come any closer to them and they were told to jump in and swim to us and we would pick them from the sea. They all wore life jackets. Only the Chief Steward objected saying that he couldn`t swim.

He was told to jump or be left behind. He jumped and splashed his way to the lifeboat and was hauled aboard. It wasn`t until we arrived in Iceland that we learned that he had hung on to an atache case with the ships papers. Because of his devotion to duty all monies spent on board ship by the crew was docked from their pay when we returned to England and the items bought went down with the ship. To crown it all the moment we left the ship our pay was stopped. My discharge book shows that I was paid off at sea. An official medical report released in 1997 stated that I was pulled out of the water semi-concious. As I was aware of what was going on I believe that I was only tired. Back home on New Years Eve as in previous years relatives and friends came to our house to welcome the New Year in. I was in their thoughts and they wondered how I was faring. Uncle Harry passed the remark that with the terrible losses of German submarines in the last few months I would be as safe as houses.

At dawn we heard the throbbing of diesel engines. The arrangement made in the event of taking to the lifeboats was put into practice until I told them that the lifeboat engine was in bits. It was then assumed that the throbbing noise we were hearing must be from a submarine. Those wearing gold braid chucked that clothing overboard. Evidently only officers were taken on board submarines as prisoners of war. Fortunately the sea troughs were very deep at least fifteen feet and none of the boats or rafts were spotted by the lookouts on the submarine nor did we see them. Just before noon an armed trawler HMS Elm came into view. This turned out to be the destroyer the airplane pilot told us to expect. Slowing down but not stopping it came alongside our lifeboat. One of the seamen grabbed hold of the scrambling net and when the swell lifted us up to deck level we jumped two at a time on to the net and hauled aboard by the waiting sailors. When the last man was safely on board the armed trawler cruised around picking up more survivors and at the end of the search it was found that the Second Mate was missing.

We were given dry toast to eat. There were now on board this tiny vessel its crew of a dozen and us forty survivors. Apart from one slice of toast I was given on arrival, I dont remember what other meals I may have had. All the sailors gave up their bunks for us and I slept for twelve hours. To keep overcrowding down to a minimum the survivors were split up into sea watches and until we reached Iceland all bunks were shared. Beds were never made and as one man left his bunk another hopped in. I shared the 12 to 4 watch with the HMS Elm 3rd engineer and was given a good insight to the workings of a triple expansion steam engine. No one washed or shaved. Each morning every man was offered a tot of rum. We returned to the scene of the attack and found that the ship was still afloat but listing badly. The HMS Bulldog was already there making a salvage attempt. In a bid to tow her to Iceland a party of sailors had boarded her and tried to secure tow lines. They failed because the sea was too rough and returned to the tugboat.

The gunners of HMS Elm fired several rounds into her double bottom tanks in an attempt to sink her but to no avail. It was then left to its fate and both naval vessels headed for Iceland.

Before we left Doxfords we were told that this would be a very difficult ship to sink which is now being proved.

I wonder what would have been the outcome if all the work had been completed before sailing to New York ?.

The book "The War At Sea"" states that MV Empire Housman was attacked this time by U545 and U744 and that it was finally sunk by the U744 a couple of days later.

The U744 was sunk after a long chase by HMS Kennilworth Castle, HMS Gatinaue, HMS Fennel, HMS Chaudiere, HMS Icarus, HMS Chilliwack and HMS St Catherine on 5 March 1944. The crew was taken prisoner. The U545 was sunk by aircraft on 10 February 1944, the crew was rescued by another U-boat

We were a scruffy looking outfit when we landed at Reykjavik in Iceland. Military lorries transported us to an American army camp where we were kitted out by the American Red Cross and then directed to a Nissen hut which we were to share with the soldiers. They came from all parts of America. One I became friendly with was from Ohio. His name was Oscar. They were in training for the Second Front now known as Overlord the invasion of Normandy which took place on 6 June 1944

It was quite an experience living with them. We were offered the same meals, shared the same billet, discipline, hardships and recreation.

Each day 3-00pm it turned dark and the snow fell continuously throughout the night stopping about 8-00am when it became light. While I was there it never snowed in the daytime. At 6-00am the night patrol visited every Nissan hut and cleared the snow from the doorways. When cleared a soldier opened the door and shouted that it was time to get up. I like the others dressed only in a singlet, shorts, slippers carried a towel and a bar of soap we made for the ablutions which were two fields away and covered with snow which had fallen in the last ten hours and it was still snowing. On our return we dressed for breakfast. The breakfast was of an unusual design made to carry a cereal, fried eggs and bacon, bread and a cup of tea.

On our last day in the camp Commander Sikorsky told us that we may leave the camp and go into Reykjavick but warned us against speaking to the Icelanders.

They were resentful of the occupation by British and American troops ignoring the fact that if we hadn`t taken it the Germans may have. We mingled with the people but because we were wearing civvies no one gave us a second glance.

The houses and other buildings were mainly built with wood. In the streets American soldiers were busy digging trenches and laying pipes in them. When the job is finished the residents in the town will have hot water and central heating in their houses, the heated water comimg from the hot springs a little way out of the town. A couple of us went to see these geysers. The streets were covered in deep snow. Leaving the town behind the snow gradually gave way to lush green grass surrounding the hot springs with the mountains in the background.

Some geysers were shooting steaming hot water up to the sky while others were just bubbling. People were spread out on the grass sun bathing. Others were languishing in the warm pools while we were muffled up to the eyes in thick warm clothing.

I would have liked to have swam in the pool but as I did not have any swimming trunks I did not go in. I never thought about going in wearing my underpants.

A GOLDEN OPPORTUNITY LOST.

Some of the crew experienced in surviving torpedoed ships elected not to accept a passage home this time but wait for another ship. Meanwhile found work on the docks.

A passage home was booked for the rest of us on a small Icelandic passenger ship the SS Lyre which was completely crewed by family members. The men worked on the bridge, engine room and deck. The women served as stewardesses and cooks. Other passengers were Icelanders and I wondered what brings them to England when they were supposed to be anti-British. We sailed next day. During the crossing an unidentified aircraft buzzed us and the air raid alarm was sounded. Everyone donned lifejackets but there were no further incidents. For the rest of the voyage we only sat around eating, sleeping and waiting. We docked at Fleetwood late in the afternoon. When through the Customs we went straight to the railway station and caught the first available train out. We changed trains at Crewe and Leeds standing in the corrodors all the way and arrived in Newcastle after midnight. There were no trains to Sunderland until next morning. At the portable snack bar we bought hot dogs and conversing with a bystander learned that a milk float was driven to Sunderland every day at 2-00am. On its arrival we asked the driver if he would take us to Sunderland. He agreed but would not accept payment saying he was only too pleased to help servicemen. As we travelled down Newcastle Rd toward the Wheat Sheaf I saw that a great change had taken place during the short time that I had been away. When I left the town a month ago a strict black-out was in force and now the street lights were on. Black-out restrictions for other lighting remained.

It was 3-00am when I knocked on my front door. My parents couldn`t believe it was me standing there. They had received a letter from the shipping company only the previous day to say that I was safe and well in a foreign port. We chatted until 6-00am then I turned in and slept until noon. I came downstairs just in time to hear Aunt Vera who had only just arrived telling Mam and Dad that she had heard from a reliable source that I was in Canada. I entered the room and said "Hello"

A letter arrived from Thornholme ARP headquarters requeting the return of my uniform now that I was no longer in the service. I returned the comeplete outfit except the battle blouse which I had taken to sea with me and was lost with the ship.

I had to pay for it. I didn`t mind that but I was none too pleased when I learned that about three months later that every ARP volunteer in the town was stood down and all were to keep the complete outfit except the tin hat and gas mask.

Later in the day I reported to the shipping office clerk in Tatham St. and was granted three weeks survivors leave in addition to earned leave at the end of which I was to report to Mr Sanderson the official in charge of the Shipping Pool based on the Newcastle Quayside where I would be offered my next berth.

From 8 December 1943 till 10 January 1944 a total of 33 days I went through an experience which I will never forget. I had not been away very long but it was enough for me to appreciate the true value of home life.

During the next few days I visited friends and relatives and at nights I went with friends to the dance halls. At the weekends to the socials at the Colliery and Sea Rd Posts not yet closed down.

Tommy Watson, Phoebe Harrison, Val Cockton and me made a foursome for a short time. At a dance in Binns Recreation Hut in Newcastle Rd. we met Olga Gray and Naomi and the foursome was changed but even this didn`t last.

CHAPTER 5

1944 TO 1945

━━━━━━━━━━━━━━━━━━━━━

At the shipping Pool I was offered three berths. The first was an oil tanker. I turned that down because that class of ship spent very little time in port and I wanted to see the world. Next was a cable ship which was quite the opposite. It could be based in one port for many months at a time so I gave it the thumbs down.

MV HOPECREST AND THE RIOT ACT

━━━━━━━━━━━━━━━━━━━━━━━━━━━━━━━

The third offered was the MV Hopecrest a general cargo ship currently in a Greenock Dock. Mr Sandersons description sounded good. It was about six years old and had tramped to many parts of the world. Another Doxford lad Billy Robinson and Joe Lawson see p49, 61 and myself agreed to join her. On the morning of 20 March the three of us met at Sunderland railway station, went to Newcastle changed trains for Glasgow arriving at 6-00pm only to learn that the last train for Greenock had departed and we were stranded. Eventually we found lodgings in 38 Eldon St. The three of us had to share the one bed. What will todays people say about that? Next morning after breakfast we found our way to Greenock and the docks and there saw in front of us a dirty, rusty looking old tramp ship. Could this be the MV Hopecrest ? It was only six years old Mr Sanderson had said.

Our hearts sank when we boarded her. The outside paintwork of the accommodation was covered in rusty patches. Worse was to follow. The inside of the engineers cabins were in a dreadful state. They were dirty and badly in need of paint and most of the furniture was battered. The junior engineers cabins were very small and double bunked. We then went in the engine room. The main engine, auxilliaries and the bulkheads were all painted a very dark green. With only two bulbs to light the area up presented a bleak and dismal picture us. Confirming Mr Sandersons description there was on the main engine above the controls a brass plaque engraved with Barclay Curle 1938

73

At first we refused to stay and threatened to go home. While discussing the situation a pompous individual probably from the local shipping office came aboard. I assumed that the captain must have sent for him. He read the Riot Act out to us and we told him what he could do with it and then said that until there was a big improvement made with the accommodation we would refuse to stay on board and go home.

He went away and we sought assistance from the local AEU. When the delegate arrived and sized up the stuation he said that he would take up our case.

The outcome of the dispute was that our living quarters would be tidied up and repairs made that same day.

It was also promised that on our return after only a six weeks voyage to Algiers and back we would be sent home on leave and return when the accommodation was properly done.. Unfortunately for us the Top Brass were making war plans which would come into effect soon and being patriotic left us with no choice but to remain but on hindsight I believe that the company was fully aware of the true situation. A squad of workers arrived and made the place clean and presentable

After finally settling in our makeshift cleaned up quarters we went ashore and found Greenock had little to offer in the way of entertainment. We learned about the Cragburn Ballroom in nearby Ashton and went there.

Most of the girls were from the WRNS station in Greenock. Our style was cramped a bit when we learned that they had to be back in their billet by midnight, but we made do.

Our experiences over the next few weeks made us wonder how the previous crew had managed to bring the ship to the Tail Of The Bank. From there tugboats would have towed the ship to this dock in Greenock. The main engine and auxilliaries were not in proper working order. After the ship had docked the crew was paid off and only the captain and the chief steward remained to sign on for another voyage.

The rules at this time did not allow anyone to sign Articles after reaching the age of sixty-five years. This will be the chief stewards third voyage each time stating his age to be sixty-five.

While our accommodation was being attended to we went home for the week-end leaving in time to catch the 4-00pm train from Glasgow. Next night I went dancing with friends at the Grange Park School and on Sunday night attended the service in the Colliery School First Aid Post. The following morning I left Sunderland at 9-00am so that I was sure of reaching Glasgow in time to catch the last train to Greenock.

When I climbed aboard I learned that the engineers were ashore leaving only the duty engineer in charge. It was too late to go in search of them so I stayed and kept him company.

Next day an attempt was made to sail up the River Clyde. All was ready. The seamen standing by were holding the mooring ropes ready to cast them from the bollards. Down below the engineers were coaxing the auxilliaries to work. The Chief was standing by the controls to start the engine and I was waiting to respond to the telegraph. It rang for slow ahead. I replied and the Chief operated the controls to start the engine. After the shaft had turned a few revolutions there was a loud bang and the engine came to a sudden stop and black smoke filled the engine room making it difficult to breathe and for a short while it was most uncomfortable. After it had cleared away p further attempts to start the engine failed. The mooring ropes remained looped over the bollards and the boat trip up the river was cancelled.

More visits to the Cragburn Ballroom seemed likely and we became quite attached to the place and the WRNs. They were rather sorry when it was time to say goodbye.

Next morning tugs arrived and towed us up the river to Henderson Dry Dock at the river end of Merkland St. where a complete survey of the engine room was to be conducted.

Serious faults were found in the main engine and auxilliary machinary. The following day the local fitters started on the long list of repairs.

There was an underground railway station in Merkland St. which we sometimes used to go to the city centre. The dock was only two or three hundred yards from the Partick main street but I found that the trams were more convenient as they ran to all parts of the city. It just so happened that the day we docked the Henderson Dock office staff had already booked the Prince of Wales Ballroom for a works dance for that night. The engineers and deck officers on our ship were invited to attend. After dancing with several partners I met Ivy Lynn one of the office workers with whom I dated several times during my stay. We danced at the Astoria where she taught me some Scottish sequence dances, one in particular "The Pride of Arran" I went to the Church of Scotland next day Easter Sunday. I was with Ivy on Easter Monday and we visited Balloch a small village on a bank of Lock Lomond.

We spent some time in a small hotel which was being built mainly to accommodate merchant seamen who when on leave were unable to go home such as those who lived in the Hebrides, Orkneys and the Shetlands. It was to be named "Atlantic Cottage". Although not yet complete it was open for high teas. One day she took me to her home to meet her sister Myrtle. For a reason known only to herself she confessed to me that she had a crush on Duncan a Canadian.

She did not corrospond with him or even know where he was. I sometimes wondered if she ever found him. After sailing we wrote to each other but it soon petered out.

When at home I was dating Doris Marshall and here in Glasgow Ivy. I had never believed in wartime romances and marriage. These and further escapedes strengthened that belief.

Mrs Aflick who lived opposite was visiting Mam when I came home one week-end and I told her that I had just arrived from Glasgow and she suggested that when I returned to my ship it would be nice if I called on her niece Maud Mushens see p43 as I had met her some years earlier and she gave me her address.

Before the war Maud had stayed with her Aunt and Uncle on a holiday and it was then when I had met and spent some time with her. After rejoining my ship I took the first opportunity to call on her at her home in Dumbarton. She introduced me to her family and I was made very welcome. There was her mother and father, her brother in law who had married her sister Rhoda and had lived with them ever since. A couple of years earlier Rhoda was killed in the blitz on Glasgow. Both men worked in the Singer motor factory. Maud was engaged to a merchant navy engineer and was expected home in the near future. He never arrived during my stay in Glasgow. I spent the evening chatting and playing card games. They taught me to play Poker. I was invited to stay overnight.

Next morning after breakfast I returned to my ship travelling in a thirty minutes tramcar ride. For the next two or three weeks we went dancing at the Locarno, roller skating at the Palais or went to a cinema. Sometimes we stayed in with the family chatting and playing cards. On each occasion I stayed overnight.

On Saturday 2nd March there was a friendly internatioal football match between Scotland and England at Hampden Park.

Before the game began Field Marshall Montgomery addressed the crowd of 33,000. He spoke about the Second Front which everyone was waiting for and was expected to be launched very soon. The crowd remained silent listening intently to his every word.

Wearing Englands colours I was one lone Englishman surrounded by dozens of Scotsmen. Every one enjoyed the game. Even though England won there was not a hint of trouble.

After another week-end at home I arrived back in Glasgow to find that the ship was no longer in Henderson Dock. I finally found her several hours later in Queens Dock in Paisley over the river which is opposite to the White Inch ferry boat landing. This ferry was just a large raft unable to transport vehicles only foot passengers. A stationary engine hauled it from one side to the other and it was very slow moving. One night after leaving Ivy. Yes I am still dating Ivy I waited at White Inch for the ferry.

It was well after midnight when I finally reached the MV Hopecrest which was in complete darkness. I thought nothing of it at the time and so as not to disturb my room mate Billy Robinson I quietly made myself ready for bed and climbed into my bunk. Next morning I learned that a major breakdown had occured just after I had gone ashore and all the other engineers had been at it until long after I had turned in. Blissfully unaware of the emergency I slept peacefully through it all.

By this time most merchant ships had Oerlickon anti-aircraft guns fitted and ours had in addition a heavy naval gun mounted on the deck aft all looked after by DEMS.

Our ship like many others at this stage of the war was taken over by the Sea Transport Office STO. and informed us that we were to take part in the Second Front invasion which later became known as the D-Day Normandy Landings. At the shipping office we were given the option of staying with our ship or be transferred to another not taking part. We all stayed and our civilian identity card was overstamped with a capital V.

Tied alongside my ship was a tank landing craft all ready for the invasion. I went aboard and talked with the RN artificer and he showed me round the engine room.

ALGIERS

We were loaded with an assortment of provisions in the holds. Secured on deck were pinnaces, tanks and lorries all fully tanked up with fuel ready to go when beached. The army drivers who were to drive these vehicles away on landing were on board. Next day we sailed down the river to Gourock at the Tail of the Bank where a convoy was being formed. Leaving Gourock we skirted the islands then headed south through the Irish Sea. As we passed Lands End it was cold and very windy which roughed up the sea. At this point the convoy turned into the English Channel but for a reason which was never disclosed to us a few vessels including ours left the main convoy and changed to a south-westerly course.

When we were about a thousand miles into the Atlantic Ocean we about turned and set a course for Gibralter. The rough sea had now moderated and being in a warmer climate our room mates came out of hibernation, cockroaches.

On the 6th June at 3-000am I saw the lights of Tangier.

At 8-00am passing Gibralter the news of the Normandy landings came over the wireless. Speculation was high. Were we bound for the south of France?.

The food being served up was very basic. For one meal in particular we were served with corned beef and vegetables. Taking it back to the galley we complained to the chief steward that some of the meat was bad. He advised us to cut the bad bits out and the rest would be all right. We scraped the meat from our plates and dropped it on the floor. The message got through. The cooking improved and no more bad meat came our way again.

Algiers from the sea looked very picturesque with its tiers of whitewashed houses on the rising slopes of the town. During the next few days I saw what it was really like. We docked on the 8th June and discharged the cargo all of it was for the NAAFI, Navy, Army, Air Force, Institute which was in effect a huge canteen run for the Forces. When the tanks and lorries were unloaded they were immediately driven away. With them gone we knew now that we were not going to France. When the landings did take place on the 8th August we were far. far away. There was a complete blackout in force here. I thought that I had seen the last of them after the restrictions back home had been eased The dock gates were manned by South African soldiers. When leaving and returning to the docks passes had to be shown and I would have word with them.

I became friendly with one and learned a lot about South Afirican customs. He was an African-Boer and had been stationed here for three years.

Just beyond the docks on the stretch of flat land were the French shops, businesses and homes. Behind them were the native quarters on the slope I had previously mentioned. I haggled and bargained with street traders for trinkets and fruit.

For soap and cigarettes or a couple of francs girls would offer their personal services. One of the streets on the slope had an entrance through an archway of Moorish design. It was named Rue d`islay.

Most of the buildings were single storeys, square with flat roofs. Those with a dome were Mosques. I saw one and a prison close by.

We visited the YMCA and the Pinder Club where we played table tennis. One of the cinemas I went in was called Cine Lux. Americn films were shown with the dialogue printed in French and Arabic along the bottom and sides of the screen. One evening I called at the Anglican Roman Catholic Church. On Sunday morning I went to St Marks Church of England. From my ship a party of DEMs marched to this church. After the service I walked back with one of the soldiers I had spent some time with in Glasgow. He was from Bury. On my return I was called before the Captain and he asked me why I had fraternised with a private soldier. I told him that I looked upon him as a friend. I then asked why was it wrong to go out wih a private soldier. Given the opportunity I would go out with my brother. He is a serving private soldier in the British Army. No satisfactory answer was given. He just mumbled that it was bad for disciplane. Interragation over.

Shop assistants were French and only knew a little bit of English. Using my eight lessons of french orals I had learned at school I had a hilarious encounter with one and finally left with a few purchases.

As I left the shop a young French/Algerian girl approached me and asked in broken English if I knew Johnny. She said that he was an American soldier she was supposed to have met an hour ago. Over here all American soldiers were known as Johnny so I guessed that she had been dumped. I stayed with her and struggled to explain that he would not show up.

On my first visit to the Casbah I saw that it was enclosed by a wall with French soldiers at the entrance gates. People were going in and out all the time. We were challenged by a soldier and when we spoke he said "Non Inglis, allez allez go" We had no choice but to leave. Those three incidents induced me to buy a French/English phrase book.

A few days later having learned a few phrases we had another try at the Casbah. This time when we were stopped I simply replied with "L`Engineurs Francais" and were waved through. Conditions in the Casbah were in stark contrast with the Fench Quarter. The streets were narrow and covered in refuse ankle deep. The majority of the people wore mucky smelly garments. I wondered how they could live like that. Some sat on the pavement smoking from Hubble bubble pipes, drinking, playing dominoes and chess. We called them WOGs. a polite expression meaning "Wily Oriental Gentlemen"

I never saw the inside of their hovels but judging from the outside I expect that they would be no better.

We left Quay Dakar and anchored in the Bay for the night. We sailed next day for Casablanca.

On the way I began to realise that even though we had been taken over by the STO and sailed with the invasion convoy those planning the campaign must still have wanted our cargo to be landed at Algiers and it must have been convenient to put us and the other few ships in that convoy without any explanations.

CASABLANCA

After three days in calm waters we sailed into Casablanca harbour and anchored. It was very cool, not what I had expected in North-West Africa. From the anchorage I was amazed to see the city ablaze with lights. That was a wonderful experience after enduring the blackout for three years back home and my time in Algiers.

Next morning we tied up at berth 22. Sea watches were changed to day work and after tea were able to go ashore. It was dark but no blackout. The street and shop lights brightened the place up and we toured the town searching out places of interest. We sampled the Cafe de France one of many restaurants then a visit to the Union Jack club in Rue Gallieni a recreation centre for the Forces where food and goods were cheaper. Transport was very ancient. Carts were pulled by one or two horses, carriages by teams of four horses along the scrupulously clean broad streets of beautiful buildings. Military vehicles and the occasional 1910 motor car were the most modern. I stood beneath a signpost that pointed to all the major capital cities of the world and I had my photo taken by a Moor.

We went to the Medina and by using the same French phrases we were not questioned at the gate. It had the same smelly aroma as in the Casbah in Algiers

I continued to practise my newly learned phrases in the shops and surprised myself with the results. After these successes I decided to buy a phrase book to use in whatever country we expected to visit. In my travels I learned a smattering of French, Arabic and Hindustani, enough to get by with.

One of the Riley boilers needed descaling and the company agent engaged local labour to do the work. To start the work it fell to me to prepare the tools, equipment and to supervise. Early in the morning I extinguished the oil fired burners, blew the water from the boiler. At the end of the day when it was safe I removed the hand hole covers at the bottom of the boiler to allow air to enter. Later I removed the man hole cover from the boiler top and left it to cool overnight. Next morning at seven I lowered a ladder in the boiler, it was still warm inside. With the tools on the floor plate all was ready.

This is how the Arab engaged to do the work tackled it.

He came down the ladder to the floor of the boiler room, looked for a suitable place for his cracket and sat on it and never moved until the boiler had been descaled. How was the boiler cleaned ?. Was he a magician and used magic ?. No he used what I believed to be his family. A woman with two boys and two girls ages ranging from ten to sixteen came down the ladder and without any attempt at modesty stripped themselves of all clothing except sandals. Three went inside the boiler and scraped the lime while one outside raked the lime from the hand holes. They each took turns at the hand holes. Soon they were so covered in lime dust it was impossible to say who was male or female. When they emerged from the boiler the Arab actually left his cracket and hosed them down. When they were dried and dressed they all left and the Arab went to collect his hard earned dirhams the local currency.

We loaded up with Phosphate then left La Grande Jetty for an anchorage where we stayed for a few days to wait for a passing convoy which we were to join.

We lay half a mile from the beach and about two hundred yards from the Mole which stretched to the beach. The gangway with three flights of steps with a platform between each flight was lowered for the benefit of the Captain and his agent.

Those platforms made excellent diving boards. Many crew members took advantage and were diving and swimming in the warm water. I swam with one to the Mole then walked to the beach, lay on the golden sands sunbathing then swam back to the ship. Among those watching the swimmers was a forty year old soldier. When we came on deck he approached us and told us he had never swam but wished he could. We suggested that he came in the water now while he was thinking about it. He borrowed a pair of swimming trunks. We held him as he slid into the sea. He then went through the motion of the breast stroke with the two of us supporting him and swam to the bow and back. He was enjoying it so we asked him if he would like to swim away from the ship. He agreed so we swam about a hundred yards then turned back. With about twenty yards to go first one then the other gently slipped the supporting arm away leaving him to swim unaided to the platform.

We told him what he had done. He thought he was being held all the time. Before we sailed for the USA he was swimming without help. He had made a life long wish come true.

One morning a terrible explosion shook the ship. My last ordeal was still in my mind and I thought we were under attack. A tanker was taking on fuel when something caused the fuel to ignite. The flames shot up a hundred feet, the smoke thousands. The fire was extinguished after ten hours fighting the blaze but the smoke hung around for much longer and there were several casualties including three dead.

A Royal Navy liberty boat ferried crew members between all ships and shore every hour from morning till midnight. Going ashore for the last time we visited the Parc Central. The trees, shrubs and flowers were well kept. I didn't see any bowling greens, tennis courts or a lake. In the evening we danced at the American Red Cross Officers Club in the Rue Chevandis de Valdome.

Next day sea watches were resumed and I was put with the Second Engineer on the four to eight watch. At five in the afternoon we sailed from the anchorage and joined the convoy from West Africa bound for London. Meanwhile another convoy had left the UK bound for the Hampden Roads Norfolk Virginia USA. and we were to join it. A couple of days later when the other convoy was sighted we slipped away and took up our new station. There were at least sixty ships a quarter mile between each vessel. The sea was calm, the sun was shining, some men off watch were sunbathing on deck. With imagination one could think that we were on a pleasure cruise. Out of sight the American escorts were circling the convoy. Now and again one would come and sail through the lines of ships probably to keep up moral.

MV HOPECREST AND THE US DESTROYER 212

Several hours after taking up station a reciprocating cooling water hose on top of the main engine burst and we had to stop to repair it. It didn`t take long. The other ships sailed on at eight knots.

The US destroyer 212 stayed behind to look after us until after the repair was made then sped off and we moved away at our full speed of twelve knots and not being too far behind we soon caught up with them. Before reaching

Chesapeake Bay on the 8th July we were to break down several times. In spite of the repairs that had been done in the Glasgow engineering works the auxilliary pumps were in a dreadful condition.

They stalled regularly but we learned that with a gentle tap with a hammer got them moving. The rods were so badly worn it was impossible to adjust the timing. This was bad enough but there were more serious defects still to come to light.

Two days later this same destroyer sailed through the convoy lines and using an Aldis lamp warned all ships to be prepared for action as submarines were reported to be in the vicinity. From then on radio silence was maintained throughout the voyage. We could listen in but not transmit. The sea was now quite rough and I felt a wee bit squeamish when I went on watch but it soon disappeared when the main engine scavenge pump failed taking us ten hours to fix it. The destroyer stayed with us until we caught up with the convoy.

We broke down again. This time a pipe joint was leaking water into the oil so we had to stop. Once again the destroyer stayed to protect us.

When the leak was stopped the destroyer escorted us back to the convoy but warned us that next time we would be left and we were to find our way to the Azores and go in for proper repairs. Sure enough we broke down with another leak. Try and imagine my feelings cooped inside the engine casing knowing that we were not being protected by the escort. When in sight of the Azores we expected to be ordered to go to Ponta Belgarda. When the expected order was not given we carried on but each time we broke down after that we were left to Providence.

Two days before reaching Chesapeake Bay the Finnish bosun warn ed us that a hurricane was brewing and orderd all hatches to be battened down.

Four hours later the radio gave out a hurricane warning and within a half hour it hit us but thanks to the bosun we were ready for it. What if we had only acted on the radio warning?

Anchoring off Norfolk we waited for a pilot to come on board to navigate us up Chesapeake Bay. That meant standby for me.

When a pump was needed and before opening the valve to set it working it was customary to drain the steam chest of water until steam came out. This method was used to heat the water for when washing clothes. The drain pipe from the pump was put into a bucket of water, opened the valve and when the water was hot enough closed the valve and commenced to wash. Washday on board was an every day event for working gear and occasionally for dress wear.

BALTIMORE

We arrived in Baltimore around noon and seeing some of the hurricane damage reminded me of the air raid damage back home. Many houses had their roofs blown off and dozens of windows were boarded up.

During the afternoon we were instructed to go in the saloon and strip off down to our socks to be examined by an army doctor before being allowed to go ashore. We stood in a semi circle waiting for him to come in. The doctor entered and using a six inch long wooden ruler SHE effectively cured those suffering from an over imaginative mind. After being passed fit the whole ships complement boarded a large motor launch and twenty minutes later we tied up at Hendersons Wharf at Thames St in the Harlem district. On landing we were taken to a studio in Baltimore St to have our photographs taken. They were affixed to US Coastguard passes and given to us. We were then left to our own devices. While we were all ashore the accommodations were fumigated.

This was the only promise honoured from several made by the Hopemount Company before sailing. The promise of a six weeks voyage was not because here we are in the USA several weeks after leaving Glasgow with orders to sail to the Mediterranean not the UK. We were still under the command of the STO.

On returning to the ship we weighed anchor and sailed to a quay close to Fort McHenry now transformed into a museum. It stood in its own grounds and when I paid it a visit there were two security men at the gate reading newspapers.

Their main interest appeared to be the funnies not the news.

Entering into conversation with them they gave me a brief historical account of the fort which I found very helpful when I went in to look around. Talking of newspapers the "Baltimore Sun" had 100 pages of news, comics, comments and advertisements. Sunday newspapers came on to the streets late on Friday nights. There was no vendor, you just helped yourself to the papers you wanted and put the money in a bowl on the pavement. A van came round at intervals to collect the cash and to leave more papers

Here the three shift system was applied to businesses, entertainment as well as industry. It was about midnight when I went to the Western Union to send a telegram home. I became very friendly with the girl on duty. Her name was Jennie Pomles born of Russian parents who had settled here after the 1917 revolution.

The shops, milk bars, beer bars, hair dressing saloons, cinemas, theatres, post offices, fruit and vegetable markets were all in full swing all open for twenty-three hours, closing any time for one hour for cleaning. The beer bars usually closed at five or six in the morning. No black-out here, bright lights everywhere and it doesn`t seem that we were in the middle of a war.

It brought me memories of peace time on a Saturday night in Sunderland town centre. All entertainments and shops had to shut no later than midnight and stay closed until Momday because back home Sunday was the Sabbath a day for church going people. Museums, pubs and clubs were only open at certain times. Traders were unable to keep perishable foods such as meat, fish and some fruits and vegetables till Monday and were keen to be rid of their stock so after eleven-o-clock prices were drastically cut and shoppers looked for bargains.

When the rota for night duty was made it was my lot to take the first turn. The night shift fitters camme aboard at 10-00pm and their gaffer asked me to waken him at 5-00am. All right but you had better get someone to call me first. He wasn`t amused.

A few days after our arrival the elderly Finnish bosun became ill and was taken to hospital in the city where he died.

Baltimore was suffering from a heatwave and it was so hot in the evening many families sat on the steps in front of their houses. Every day an ice cream van pulled up alongside our ship and the vendor done roaring trade. This was my first taste of ice-cream since the early days of the war.

One day I was in the town with the Second Engineer and he believing that I was too young to understand he told me to stay outside while he went in the shop to buy some tampax for his wife. Like many other products this one was unobtainable back home.

The Coney Island Grill was where I saw the biggest beefsteak sandwich ever and as I write I am still waiting to see another to match it outside of the USA.

Public transport was by street car and all destinations could be reached for a standard fare of 5 cents, 2.5 new pence, sixpence in old money.

We visited the Oasis club in Baltimore St. A black man was performing a song and dance routine in the middle of the dance floor and when he finished coins were thrown to him. I am finding these clubs and pubs are very different to those at home.

One Sunday afternoon I visited Clifton Park and on the night with others attended the Gospel Tabernacle in Wolfe St. It was packed full. A band played hymn tunes in rag time. Listening to the preachers sermon I came to the conclusion that he didn`t like the Russians. Before the service came to a close he called sinners to come to the front and repent. Most of the congregation moved forward, not us, we were wearing our best haloes shining ever so bright. I had seen nothing like this before. Shortly after leaving the Church there was a terrific thunder storm which caused a lot of damage to property.

There were several cinemas one of them being Leow Century Cinema and dozens of drug stores which were a cross between a grocer shop and an ice-cream parlour and when ashore I always called in one.

The Merchant Navy Club in Southern St. was a popular venue. A juke box played records and we danced to them, the fox trot, the quick step, the modern and old fashioned waltz , the tango and many other dances. The hostesses were very friendly. There was Shirley Westcott born in Baltimore, her father was English, her mother German. Another was Marion Krzack also born in Baltimore. Her parents emigrated from Poland after the Great War 1914-1918 and opened a grocery business. Marion was engaged to a Merchant Navy Engineer currently with the MV Eastern Prince whom she had met at this club. His home address was General Havelock Rd Ford Estate Sunderland. Two years later they were married. When I left the MN in 1947

I returned to Doxfords to work and one dinner time I was going through the gate and who should I meet coming in? None other than Marion Krzack hoping to meet some of her friends she made in the Merchant Navy Club and are now working here in Doxfords.

It was very racist here. One evening walking along Baltimore St. a white woman crossed the road and came to me and suggested that I should cross over to the other side which is reserved for white people only. She re-crossed and not being racist I just carried on walking as before.

I must have looked and dressed very English like because on the Baltimore Viaduct I was stopped by a middle aged man who asked if I was English. On replying yes he said that he was of German descent and became very aggressive as he put over his point of view about the war.

His attitude changed when I explained what it was like to be involved in air raids and sea warfare. After several minutes we parted without coming to blows and I believe he was an enlightened man over the realities and horrors of war.

One afternoon Sid and I went to a big department store similar in style to Kennedys, Joplings and Binns to buy presents to take home. Its name was The Hub.

Using the shop girl as a model I bought silk stockings, underwear, table cloths, wine glasses, a tea set and a pair of white linen sheets all unobtainable back home. I handed a fistful of dollars to the assistant and she asked me if I had a penny. It so happened that I had a couple in my pocket and I gave her one. I thought that from our conversation she had guessed that we were English and wanted one as a souvenir. She explained that in USA a penny was the term given to a cent and she wanted one to reduce the number of coins in my change.

We had a good laugh over it and I gave her two English pennies for mementoes.

In the course of our little pantomime we learned that her name was Lillian Jackson and that her mother originated from Tow Law and her father from Spennymoor. He had worked in a local pit. After the 1926 pitmans strike the family emigrated to the USA and settled in Baltimore. Her father then set himself up in business as a barber in Washington Boulevard where they now live. She invited us to her home to meet her parents and we found that they had not been fully Americanised. Their home was typically English with a scullery and a kitchen cum living room heated by a coal fire. It was in contrast to Marion Krzack home which was centrally heated from a solid fuel stove in the basement. The four of us spent our last night in Shirleys home in Johnson

Square before returning to our ship skint. I`m looking forward to some time at sea to build up my bank balance.

Next morning we sailed for the Hampden Roads. The main engine and auxilliaries had now been overhauled for the second time in just a few weeks. Time will tell if they have improved. On arrival we anchored and when not on watch a lot of our time was spent swimming and diving from the deck which because we now carry a full cargoe of provisions for Alexandria Egypt it is now only eighteen feet above the water. We were there for four days before our sailing orders came through. At last the convoy was on the move but no sooner were we out of sight of land than several planes of the American Air Force flew over the ships and used them for dive bombing practice. They dropped smoke canisters all around the ships. When the exercise was over the planes returned to their base and the smoke cleared.

The sea was calm, the sun was shining and it was a pleasure to be on deck. Then came a submarine warning and the escorts were darting all over dropping depth charges to remind us that this was not a pleasure cruise.

From a ship sailing parallel to us came a greetings message for me via the Aldis lamp. It was from Walter Knox see p30, 39 an engineer on the MV Trevotha. We had played school rugby against each other, both worked at Doxford and in the Colliery FAP.

We slept out on deck for a few nights it was so hot. When the sea was roughed up by a howling wind we stuck it out for one more night but the weather worsened and we brought our mattresses inside. A week later the sea had calmed down and we slept on deck again until we were within one day sailing of Gibralter and we returned to our cabins. There was a thunder storm as we passed through the Straits of Gibralter and at the same time several ships joined our convoy. They created a problem for us. A convoy always sail at the speed of the slowest ship and these ships were very slow.

Our slow was faster than their top speed. The only way to keep a reasonable station was to go slow, stop then slow again and repeat the process. Our engine was designed to avoid that critical speed for safety reasons.

The danger was that no more than 440yards separated us from the nearest ship at best. I expect that other ships suffered from the same problem.

A couple of days later I could just see Algiers on the horizon and while thinking of my time there my thoughts were rudely shattered as the fire alarm went off. A fire had broken out below the floor plates in the boiler room. By the time it was extinguished we had left Algiers far behind.

I was off watch and on deck as we aproached the Island of Pantelleria. We were so close I could see the people walking along the streets.

87

Until a year ago these same people were our enemies and I thought how ridiculouse it was that they are now our allies.

Over the radio came the news that Romania and Bulgaria had opted out of the war and were asking for an armistice.

ALEXANDRIA

We anchored just off Alexandria very early on the 7th September.

Gertie Gray a member of Sea Rd FAP was married to a soldier and as far as she knew he was somewhere out here in the Middle East. During my last leave when at the FAP social evening she gave me his army address hoping that that I would be able to meet up with him. On my first day ashore I made enquiries at an Army Post and was told that he had recently left for Palestine and was given his new address.

While ashore another ship tied up alongside and two of her engineers came aboard and enquired after me. They were Harry Salt and Gordon Sands both workmates from Doxfords. They waited for me in my cabin until I returned. Unfortunately this was a dry ship and I was unable to offer any strong refreshments. Before returning to their ship we had a good chin wag. That was our last meeting. After the war ended Harry went south to live and Gordon emigrated to Canada.

Next day was a sad one for Ted Kennedy. Among his mail was a letter with news of his fathers death. He was a Roman Catholic and he spent the rest of the day in his cabin praying with his rosary.

Soon after our arrival outside of the city two WRNs were murdered and their breasts cut off. Heeding official advice from the Consul Office I confined my excursions within the city limits. One night we visited the YMCA, Montgomery House Club and the Top Hat Club. On our return to the ship Paddy one of the sailors was very drunk and when crossing the gangway stumbled and fell into the water. We pulled him out, dried and put him to bed. Next morning he was surprised to learn what had happened.

On our first Sunday Sid and me went to St Marks Church for the morning service then called at th YMCA. We stayed and enjoyed a decent meal thereby missing a meal on board then off to the Merchant Navy Club. There couldn`t be a better place than this to remind me of home but I was looking for something more exotic which was not to be found here. For the next three hours we toured the city taking in Pompey Pillar and the Roman Baths then the native quarters which were no beter or worse than Casablanca or Algiers. To enter I did not have to use French phrases, there were no walls. On our way back we were stopped by shoeshine boys who insisted on polishing our shoes.

We did not want them cleaning and said so. One of them threw boot polish on our white shirts. We did not stand for that and promptly floored him and found ourselves in a fight against the odds.

Fortunately Coming out of the Top Hat Club was a group of service men one who shouted "Navy" through the doorway and within a minute more came out to join the fray.

Another time on our way to visit the catacombs we witnessed a wedding which was a very gay affair.

We also saw a rather sombre funeral. On reaching our destination I counted 99 steps down to this creepy burial ground where the coffins lay side by side in numerous tunnels.

We visited the Zoological Gardens where there were lions, tigers, bears, snakes, monkeys, gazelle, deer, storks, swans, lizards, chamaleons and white rats.

Sid Larson, Bernard Ford our Deck Apprentice from South Shields and myself volunteered to take the crews letters to the Fleet Mail Office at Ras-El-Tine to be posted home and to collect any that may be there. At the dock we boarded a Felucca, a native sailing boat which took us to our destination a few miles along the coast. There wasn`t any mail so we had a look round the area then booked a taxi to bring us back to Mohammed Ali Square a short distance from the docks. While travelling I saw many fine buildings. It is incredible that in these African countries that I have visited there are many beautiful buildings in one district and squalid shanty towns in another.

One afternoon I went on a six mile walk. Leaving the dock at gate 21 I made my way to the coast road and followed it to Ras-El-Tine then on to Port Est eventually arriving at the statue of Ismail Pasha at the end of the promenade Dela Reine Nazli. Further along was the Place Ismail leading to Mohammed Ali Square then on to Rue Soeurs (Sister St) In this street many crafts and professions were practised including the oldest one. In the open fronted shops craftsmen were working on wood, brass and leather goods. Behind these workshops were the brothels and peep shows. One of the shows was of the Donkey and the Lady. Sitting on the pavements were crippled men, women and children begging alms. We often chatted with Murphy the night watchman. He was an Arab and claimed to have been born in South Shields which he said was the true capital of Islam. He told us that all the cripples begging alms in the streets were deliberately deformed at birth to ensure that they followed the Beggar Profession

Another service at St Marks. Dinner at the YMCA then swimming in the open air pool at Sidi Bisha about a 45minutes tram ride out of town. We hitched a lift back to the docks in a RN truck driven by a Greek sailor then went to a movie. It was dark when we came out and we got lost in the maze of alleyways in the native quarter but eventually found Cairo Station and there boarded a tram which transported us to Ramleh Station only a short distance from the docks. Slowly wandering back I marvelled at the way that Ramadan was being celebrated. The people fasted from sunrise till sunset and I saw that the street kitchens were doing a roaring trade. The streets were dimly lit by oil lamps and the curling smoke from them mingled with the cooking smells and created an aroma which drifted on and on. I don`t think anyone went home hungry.

My three weeks stay in Alexandria was most enjoyable. My only regret was that I was too cautious and did not visit Cairo, the Pyramids and the desert. The chance never came my way again.

We sailed for Haifa alone unescorted on 25 September

HAIFA AND NAZARETH

Sailing close to the Palestinian coast and being off duty I had a good view of Tel-Aviv and the hotels along the coast. Another forty-one years was to pass before I was to see them again.

Approaching Haifa I saw a panoramic view of the town at the foot of Mount Carmel. It made a very pleasant picture.

Billy Robinson had a brother in the Army currently serving in the Lebanon and he had written to him a couple of weeks ago. They had not seen each other for three years and here he was at Number 7 quay waiting for the ship to tie up.

They were lucky to meet.

Before being allowed to go ashore we all had to be inoculated against Bubonic Plague which was reported to be raging throughout the country. Going ashore I expected to see carts collecting the dead such was the lecture given us concerning the epidemic. I saw no evidence of it at any time in the week that I was here and I had toured around quite a bit.

I called at an Army Post for news of Private Gray and was told he was in the Lebanon. I never met him.

There appeared to be two types of people here. Darkskinned Arabs and immigrants from Eastern Europe who first settled in the 1800s and founded Tel-Aviv. Many more were to follow in the 1900s

Among my mail was a letter from my pal Tommy Watson with whom I had made a pact not to marry until after the war. He had met Ann an ATS girl from Aberdeen and his lights went out and they are going to be married in October.

There was a strong English flavour here, red pillar boxes, English street names and signs.

It was Sunday and I had the day off. What could be better than a bit of exploring?. No one would come with me. They thought going to Nazareth was too ambitious. So off I went. On the road I met two Yanks Mr Rabbi 4th Engineer and Moems Deck Apprentice from the SS Fort Aclavick. Like me they were out sightseeing and we teamed up. We hitched lifts on an army lorry then another and were dropped off in Nazareth. From the roadside I looked in the carpenters shop where Jesus was reputed to have worked.

Leaving Nazareth we walked along the road through the wilderness of sand, scrub and stones and then headed for the Sea of Galilee. Then along came a rickety old bus full of Arabs. Stopping the bus I practised my Arabic phrases on the driver with reasonable success. We climbed on board and I chatted with the passenger. No it wasn't easy but enjoyable. It was a remarkable journey and so were the sights. Winding our way up and down hills on very narrow roads some of which were fairly good made of hard earth and stones. There were stretches of road that had sheer drops of several hundred feet at one side. From these vantage points there were wonderful views. I have not seen so many stones to the square yard as in this country. Looking at the countryside I felt that I was in a time warp. The scenes that I was looking at were exactly like the pictures in the Holy Bible. Out in the fields were shepherds tending their flocks. They wore the same type of clothing their forbears did a thousand years earlier.

There were camel caravans, women drawing water from wells then carrying the full pitchers on their heads to the tents nearby. The few houses I saw in this area were of wood, stones and clay.

TIBERIUS AND THE SEA OF GALILEE

On reaching Tiberius we bade farewell to the friendly driver and passengers. We had lunch in a cafe owned by a man who had emigrated from Venezuela. We then walked along the shore until we arrived at the Lido in the Sea of

Galilee. We found the water was so fresh it was hard work swimming but it was exhilarating. I gathered a few willicks to take home for my Mam.

The Sea of Galilee was 700ft below sea level and after climbing the steps to the road at the top we saw hill on the other side which at a guess would be about 1000feet.

We climbed to its summit, looked across and down to the lake 1700ft below. What a view. Scrambling down to the road we were lucky to hitch a lift right into Haifa

At the dock my American friends invited me aboard their vessel and to my surprise I met two ex-shipmates from the MV Empire Housman, Bob Sugarman and Ron Taylor who are now crew members of this vessel.

It was my turn for night duty. There was no cargo handling so the winches were idle and all was well in the engine room with a stoker keeping an eye on things. The other engineers were all ashore. I settled down to some writing. When finished I took my letters to the Post Office and dropped them in the pillar box close to the dock entrance and I returned to my berth. All was quiet so I nipped into bed. Next morning I learned that some time during the night that the Stern gang who were fighting for independance from Britain blew the Post Office up, not the pillar box. I heard nothing.

At the market I bought grapefruits and oranges and with them filled two kit-bags . I was certain that they would be a welcome addition to the rations. These and all the other goods that I had bought in Baltimore together with what Billy Robinson had bought almost filled our cabin leaving just a narrow path to the door.

GIBRALTER AND SWANSEA

We sailed from Haifa on Wednesday 4 October again with no escort and arrived in Port Said next day and anchored in the bay. Viewing the beach from the ship it appeared to be very sandy and free from stones but I was unable to go ashore and test it out as we only stayed for 28 hours.

The war was still very much on but once again we left port alone, not in convoy, this time bound for Swansea We sailed past the statue of Ferdinand de Lessops the Frenchman who had designed the Suez Canal.

After cruising along in warm sunshine for a couple of days the weather changed suddenly. The evening turned very cool and turned pitch black. As we were passing Malta a thunder storm developed with the rain lashing down. One of the lightning flashes revealed a ship bearing down on our beam. Both ships were blacked out.

Fortunately the officer on watch saw it and immediately telegraphed for full speed ahead and we narrowly avoided being rammed. Next day the weather turned hot and very windy causing the sea to heave.

It was dark when we dropped anchor in Gibralter Bay. I was still on watch when finished with engines was rung and I was left alone in the engine room. The bilge water was up to the floor plates. I started the pump but instead of the water going overboard it continued to rise above the floor plates.

The strum was choked and to clean it I had to go under the surface to reach the strum and rake the sediment out.

While I was submerged a depth charge exploded in the bay. Try and imagine my reaction with the memory of the MV Housman still fresh in my mind. I was up on deck in a flash. The other engineers thought it was a huge joke. Until then I was not aware that the Royal Navy patrol boats dropped depth charges every twenty minutes and searchlights were continually sweeping the bay to deter frogmen from planting limpet mines on the ships in the harbour.

Spain was neutral but it was well known that German frogmen were based there and that Germany had helped General Franco to win the Spanish Civil War in 1936.

Next morning I went on deck and being so close to the Spanish shore I clearly saw the thatched white cottages and people walking about.

After taking on bunkers we sailed into the Atlantic and along the Portuguase coast still very much on our own. As we neared the Bay of Biscay we received a submarine warning but we arrived in the Bristol Channel without incidents.

We tied up in the King's Dock in Swansea and we were there for more than three weeks discharging our cargo of one million jerry cans. It rained ever day and it was cold. I phoned home to let my parents know that I was in Swansea and I would be coming home at the week-end. We found the Merchant Navy Club to be rather tame and we only visited it once. The ship's company was invited to the ATS 623 Battery dance in Ashleigh Rd. We all had a good time. A night at the flicks then another visit to the ATS dance hall and I became friendly with a corporal just returned from her honeymoon. At the end of the evening I walked her back to the dormitary and stood chatting in the doorway. Some girls were already in bed others were in various stages of undress none of whom seemed a bit concerned of my presence in the domitary.

The Patti Pavilion was another dance hall where we met Rachel Davies and Pat Walsh and dated them a couple of times.

All shore leave was cancelled when the ship moved to the Oil Wharf in the Queen's Dock to take on bunkers then put to sea but at tea-time the order was changed to sail on the next day's high tide but the curfew was not lifted.

We had intended to go to the ATS dance that night so we sneaked off the ship and not having a pass to leave the dock we were forced to cross several railway tracks and then clamber over the dock wall. We spent the evening with the corporal and two NAAFI girls Myra and Lily. After the dance back over the wall, crossed the railway lines and on board ship. Our absence went by unnoticed.

After a wet but enjoyable stay in Swansea we sailed next day for Barrow in Furness

BARROW IN FURNESS

On the way we were enveloped in fog. We dropped anchor and waited for it to lift then it was full speed ahead at 13 knots. The engine room machinery was in much better shape than when we first joined her. As we were approaching Barrow we sailed innto very bad weather and for one terrifying moment the ship heeled over sending everything that was loose crashing to the deck.

Being close to our destination and the sea too rough to drop annchor we cruised in circles for several hours waiting for the sea to calm down sufficiently to proceed. At last we were able to make progress and when the shore was in sight we stopped and dropped anchor and waited for the pilot. As he was climbing aboard the anchor was raised. He then took charge and piloted us into Ramsden Dock

After docking the Captain refused to pay off the crew but I was able to home for the week-end and I went to visit my friend Tommy Watson and his bride Ann and they now live in a colliery house in Richmond St. near the pit.

I called on my Uncle Dave who happened to be on leave.

On my return to Barrow an RAF Officer came on board and offered the Officers a flight in an Anson trainer plane. Only two of us accepted the chance. Next day we were taken to the airfield in an RAF lorry.

After a bumpy ride I boarded the aircraft and with a struggle I squeezed myself round the machine gun and into the cockpit thinking to myself how difficult it would be for the gunner to bale out in an ermergency. After strapping myself in I waited for the plane to take off but when I looked out I only saw the sky.

I then looked at the altimeter and saw that were already at 500ft. I had not felt anything at all as the plane sped along the runway and then rising into the air. The ride in the lorry was very much rougher. We flew low over the MV Hopecrest, the RAF station on Walney Island then up and down the coast. If it had been better weather the pilot would have flown us over the Lake District. At 220mph we climbed to 2000ft well above the low lying clouds which looked like a carpet of cotton wool stretching from one horizon to another. In the river was the destroyer HMS Hardy. This was the third ship to have this name. The first was beached in the battle at Narvick Norway in 1940. The second was torpedoed and sunk in the Barents Sea some time later.

I was here only a few days so I had little time to become familiar with the town. I never found a dance hall and the only cinema available exhibited two shows a night which had to be booked before going in. It was no livelier here than in Greenock.

We sailed bound for Birkenhead and arrived in the Mersey Estuary on Saturday afternoon in thick fog and being unable to see our way to the dock we dropped anchor.

The Chief Steward expecting the crew to be paid off when we docked had allowed all food supplies to dwindle. The store room was almost empty. On Sunday the fog worsened. It was now a real pea souper and the ships agent had to engage a small boat to bring us emergency supplies. On Tuesday afternoon the fog cleared and we were able to enter Camell Lairds dry dock in Birkenhead. We were paid off at 7-00pm and booked a taxi which took us through the Mersey Tunnel to Liverpool.

We enjoyed a decent meal in the Ocean Club and then at 10-40pm went to the railway station for a train to take us home. We had to change trains at Crewe, York and Durham. It was too early for a connection at Durham so we stayed on the station platform and slept on a bench until the first train for Sunderland arrived. I reached home at 9-00am and so ended my second trip to sea.

Over Xmas I done the usual rounds of visiting relatives, friends and dancing.

1945

HOME AND THE MV WELSH PRINCE

During the New Year festivities there were parties and dancing at different Halls.

I spent most of my time visiting and going out with friends from the dance halls.

At the Newcastle Pool I was offered a berth on the MV Welsh Prince a sister ship to the Empire Housman. Most of the crew had re-signed which was promising.

I took a chance and travelled up to Edinburgh where I signed Articles. The officers quarters as expected were amidship. The all Indian crew lived aft.

A stiff climb up the one mile bank from the dock brough me to Holyrood House at this end of the Royal Mile. There were times when Royalty occupied it but when I looked through the building it resembled a museum rather than a residence. At the other end of this road was Edinburgh Castle. Parallel was Rose St famous for the large number pubs along its length.

I teamed up with John Ellis the 3rd Wireless Operator. He was younger than me by a couple of years. He like me was a survivor of a sinking. He had taken part in the Normandy landings and while anchored off the Normandy coast enemy frogmen placed limpet mines on the hull of his ship. When they detonated the ship settled on the sea bed. During the next sixteen months we shared many adventures.

Our destination was Calcutta. Leaving Leith we sailed south and overtook a small slow moving vessel. Signals were exchanged and we learned that it was bound for Bombay.

Then through the English Channel into the Atlantic Ocean. There was a heavy swell while crossing between Brest and La Corunna outside of the Bay of Biscay. Our first port of call was to be Gibralter where were to have our fresh water tanks filled. We were now in the Meditteranean and going through the narrow waters between Sicily and Tunisia we passed close to the island of Pantellaria now no longer an enemy but an ally with British troops on the island. The town lay at the foot of a mountain which seemed to cover the whole island.

Next stop was an anchorage at Port Said where dozens of bum boats swarmed around us the Gypoes trying to flog us merchandise, clothing, fruits, watches and all kinds of trinkets. sew sew girls offering to repair clothing and other ladies putting themslves on offer.

The Suez Canal is nearly a hundred miles long connecting the Mediterranean Sea to the Red Sea. Taking up station in a long line of ships we finally entered the canal which passed through the Sinai Desert. British troops were camped every few miles along its west bank.

A few miles on at Ismalia on the east bank was the marvellous palace of the then King Farouk of Egypt. The Suez Canal is too narrow to allow two ships to pass each other so a procedure was followed. When the first line of ships arrived at trhe Bitter Lakes about midway along its length they dropped anchor then waited for the ships sailing in the opposite direction to pass by the lake and continue to sail on.

When all ships have passed, the first lot left the lake and sailed for Suez. Without stops the average time to sail through the canal is twelve hours. Leaving the canal at Suez we entered the Red Sea and because Italy once the enemy and now is an ally a peaceful passage along the coast of Italian Somaliland was expected.

It was very hot and a few of us were sun-bathing on deck when the silence was shattered by a loud explosion and a column of water hurtled skywards about a hundred yards behind us. The cruiser HMS Sheffield was a mile astern and after firing that first salvo radioed this message "Don`t worry we are only practising with dummy shells." Even so I don`t think it would be very nice being hit by a dummy shell. The exercise went on all afternoon.

It was stinking hot when we reached Aden. At a hundred and forty degrees Fahrenheit in the engine room it was cooler there than on deck in the shade.

We berthed at the Oil Terminal and took on bunkers. From the deck I saw Crater the town at the foot of an extinct volcano. Four hours later we sailed non stop to the Calcutta Roads.

We rounded Ceylon, changed course and the further north we went the cooler it became. The voyage from Leith to the Calcutta Roads took forty-two days enjoying favourable weather and no enemy action.

Depending on the type of cargo being carried, a ship could expect to lie at anchor in the Roads for a very long time before given clearance to enter port but always to be ready to sail. We dropped anchor near a Liberty class vessel. After two days we were given permission to go in. A request message from the Yanks asked how after only two days we were allowed to go in. Our reply was that we carried a top prority cargo of NAAFI stores and we were looking forward to a spell ashore in Calcutta.

Their reply astounded us "Thanks we thought we were lying off Madras." As we prepared to sail into the River Hoogli I saw the American weigh anchor, turn and head south. When docked the Indian crew having come to the end of their two year voyage were paid off and they returned to their homes

CALCUTTA

A new crew was signed on. They brought with them animals and fowl and the deck aft resembled a farm yard. During this part of the voyage I learned a lot about Muslim customs. They ate meat only if they prepared it themselves and five times day knelt on a prayer mat facing Mecca in the East and prayed. Most of them were farmers having left their wives behind to look after the farms while the men were away earning extra money. They usually sailed on a two year voyage, go home then another voyage. After about ten years gave up sea life and work the farm for good.

The Serang was in command with Tindle his deputy over the engine room crew of Indians. A similar group of Indians worked on deck. This new Indian crew turned out to be a better class of people than the last lot. My work put me in close contact with them and I found these to be good natured and friendly but sometimes difficult when they conveniently couldn`t understand the English language when given a dirty job to do. From the start I got on well with the Serang, the Tindle and Storekeeper. who spoke reasonable English. They took me in hand and taught me to speak Hindustani phrases. I already posessed a phrase book. Now being able to talk with them in their own dialect I was able to delegate work without hearing "Me no savvySahib"

I was not a lover of curry. I always refused it when it was offered. The Serang noticed this and after some persuasion he managed to get me to try some in the privicy of my own cabin. I now make my own curried dishes.

The climate here in January is similar to our middle Spring so long trousers were worn when I went ashore with John Ellis and walked along Chowringee the main street. It was nearly a mile long. There were buildings at one side only and in it were shops, cinema, theatre, restaurants, tombola hall, YMCA and Service clubs. On the pavement were shoe-shine boys, a blind beggar begging for alms in the name of Allah, a figure to be seen every day. At the other side was the Maidan a wide open expanse of green common spreading down to the River Hoogli. It stretched from the docks and went far beyond the end of Chowringee.

Walking along Chowringee I saw in a shop the Indian version of Monopoly. I bought it and added it to the collection of cards, draughts, dominoes and books used by off duty officers in the saloon when it is not being used for meals.

Also to be seen were hundreds of Yanks parading up and down wearing their smart uniforms. The road was choked with horse drawn taxis, gharries and coolies pulling rickshaws, an assortment of old fashioned motor cars, ancient London buses, lorries and taxis. Horns were being honked continuously what a din.

Cows considered to be sacred wandered about the streets unhindered, all traffic giving way to them. Tramcars were in tandem, fare paying passengers rode in the first tram only, crowds filled the second, some stood on the running boards and many lay on the roof. Taxis were just as bad, they too were overcrowdered. In the streets off Chowringee were three cinemas, Metro, Odeon and the Lighthouse. Nearby was the General Post Ofice. It stood on the site of the Black Hole of Calcutta. A few minutes walk from here was the Hindu Jain Temple

From early morning till late evening the area was bustling with crowds of men in their flowing white robes. I marvelled at how white they were. They never seemed to get dirty. The few Hindu women seen outside were covered from head to feet and wore a yashmack with only the eyes visible. Most of the women seen outdoors were Eurasians and were greatly outnumbered by the men.

On the opposite bank was the town of Howrah with a bridge connecting the two towns. This bridge was only a few feet above the river with vultures perched on the girders looking very sinister as they waited to pounce on any corpse that came floating along. Every day a dead animal or a person would drift down.

To me it looked as though no attempts were made to retrieve them. Pollution was so bad we received a note from the British Embassy warning us to attend hospital for treatment if we ever fell in the river.

Every day thousands would cross over this bridge, probably going to work in the Howrah Jute Mills which exported huge quantities of jute all over the world. The scene reminded me of the crowds crossing the Wearmouth Bridge after a football match at Roker Park.

Beyond the outskirts of Calcutta and as far as I could see the countryside was barren of trees and bushes yet I was told that at the start of the 20th century the jungle came right up to the edge of the town which would have been much smaller than it is now in 1945

After a short stay we sailed bound for the UK. After we left the Arabian Sea and entered the Gulf of Aden we met the slow boat again. It was still chugging on its way to Bombay. We exchanged messages which included the current hit song " I`d like to get you on a slow boat to China", We sailed on through the Red Sea, the Suez Canal and into the Mediterranean.

VE Day 8th May 1945 the war in Europe came to a close but we received orders to continue sailing under wartime conditions because it was feared that some submarine commanders may not be aware that the war was over.

DUNDEE

Following us into the Dundee docks was a U-boat being escorted in by a destroyer. Already moored there were several U-boats that had surrended earlier.

We were given seven days leave knowing that on our return we were to take part in the invasion of Malaya or Singapore. I spent only one night here so I learned very little about the town. This marks the end of my first voyage on the MV Welsh Prince.

HOME

I caught the train early next morning and as it steamed over the Tay and Forth Bridges I was thrilled with the experience of crossing such long bridges.

I spent my leave calling on relatives and friends. One night Mam, Dad, Uncles, Aunts and Cousins all met in Grandmas house. Leaving the women in the house Granda and the other men went to the Wheat Sheaf pub to celebrate the end of the war in Europe. We were rationed to one pint only so we caught a tramcar to Roker. Walked back to the Wolsely. Only half of us were served as there was a shortage of glasses. The rest went to the Derby near by and found themselves in the same situation. We stayed until our glasses were empty. We left and returned to the Wolsely with our empty glasses.and continued our revelry. I am not too certain as to the rest of the evening but it was unlikely for any of us to get tipsy due to the shortage of glasses and beer.

Other nights I went dancing at the Colliery FAP, the Rink and Wetheralls. One day Mrs Douglass a neighbour from down the street called in and in conversation I told her that I was going back east again. She then asked if I would take a birthday cake back with me and hopefully give it to her son Harry for his 21st birthday in a few weeks time.

He is in the RAF and is stationed somewhere in the East but don`t bring the cake back, share it with your friends if you not meet him. I told her I would take it but the chances of meeting up with are slim. I then told her that last year I had tried to contact a soldier in the Middle East but failed.

A few days later I returned to Dundee with the cake. It was very late when I finally got on board. On reaching my cabin I found it was locked from the inside. It was common practice for relieving engineers to take over a cabin of an engineer away on leave so I went to the 4ths room next door. It was open so I crept in without disturbing the sleeper and quietly lay on the settee and went to sleep. Next morning I woke up to hear a female voice say " Hans I think there is someone in our room" The couple whos privacy I had invaded the previous night was the 6th engineer Hans Bulmer and his wife. At mid-day Mrs Bulmer and the relieving engineer who had occupied my room left the ship to go home. Those of us who had not signed Articles made their way to the Shipping Office to do so. When I returned I asked Mr Bradford the Chief Steward to look after the birthday cake. I then told him the tale behind the cake. He thought it most unlikely that Harry would get it and we should tuck into it now. I told him that I believed in miracles but if I fail to meet up with him the cake would go on the table when we sail from Calcutta. Next day saw us on our way to take part in the invasion of Malaya or Singapore. Our cargo of war materials, tanks, lorries, jeeps, pinnaces and light ammunition. We followed the same course as the previous voyage enjoying 42 days of good weather and calm seas to reach the Calcutta Roads. We did not meet the slow boat so we assumed it must now be in Bombay.

MV Welsh Prince Second Voyage

CALCUTTA AND MADRAS

This time there were no ships lying off the coast and we sailed straight into Calcutta.

my friend John Ellis and me went ashore and walked along Chowringee to the residential area. Passing Park St. I happened to see an army office, so taking a chance I went in and gave the sergeant at the desk a note with an address something like this:-

L/Ac H Douglass 1234567 nth Battalion SEAC.

He took the paper away and five minutes later came back and said that we were in luck and that our friend had arrived only three weeks ago from Rangoon and was now only five miles up he road in a transit camp awaiting a new posting. The sergeant said that he would arrange it for him to be at this office at 6-00pm next day. Thanking the sergeant we left and continued our walk about. When we were back on board I told Brad that I was to meet Harry at six-o-clock next day and that set in motion preparations for a birthday party. The following evening when we returned to that office I got a big surprise because waiting with Harry was a soldier from Sunderland he had only recently befriended. This soldier was George Buckley a friend of mine. We had served together on the Colliery School FAP before he joined the army. After a lot of chin wagging we toured the town.

The next evening we picked them both up and brought them back to the ship for a party with Harry the guest of honour on his twenty-first birthday.

Most of the deck, engineers and radio officers were present. Brad brought the cake along and it went down well. It had been a big one but not a crumb was left. Booze was in plenty, not like on the MV Hopecrest. Harry`s mother was pleased as punch when at a later date she learned that not only had I found him but we were in time to hold a party for him on his actual birthday.

During the six weeks waiting for the invasion John and myself were able to meet Harry and George many times. Every night out together we would end up at the Monica Cafe and have a slap up supper. I was never certain whether the eggs we ate were from hens, snakes or alligators but I suffered no ill effects.

Derek Alderson`s father see p14 was a marine engineer and I met him when his ship was moored alongside mine in the invasion fleet here in Calcutta. It was our first meeting and it was only through conversation that I realised the connection.

The merchant ships were moored three abreast across the River Hoogli and stretched a mile or more along its length awaiting the order to sail and invade Malaya. Dramatically Japan surrendered and orders were changed. Instead of the ships sailing as an invasion fleet all were deployed to different ports. Our orders were to go to Madras and await further orders. Before sailing we had one more party on board and a final fling ashore with Harry and George.

We were in Madras for only a few days waiting for a convoy to be assembled. During this time a football match was arranged between our ships company and the Madras Tigers a local football club. Our team of eleven was chosen from eighteen officers. We could not all play as the ship had to be manned to cover normal duties. The men over fifty volunteered to keep watch aboard while the match was being played. We played with a laced leather caseball. Our strips were white shorts, shirts and ordinary or engine room shoes. The Tigers wore brightly coloured shorts, shirts and played barefooted.

I began the game in goal saving several before letting in two. I then played on the right wing but did not score any goals

The final score The Tigers 5-2 MV Welsh Prince

Eager to explore the city I stopped a policeman and speaking Hindustani I asked him the way to the park.

Having just completed his tour of duty he offered to walk with me, as his house was on the way to the park. As we walked I practised my phrases on him fairly successfully . I was pleased with my efforts.

When we reached his house he invited me in for a cup of tea. I was amazed at the interior. The room was decorated in bright red, green and other gaudy colours. We sat on cushions. There were no chairs and no table. We talked for nearly an hour while drinking tea from tiny brass cups served from an ornamental brass teapot. As was the custom his wife remained in the back room and I only saw her briefly when she served tea and cleared away. I thanked him for his hospitality, took my leave and within minutes I arrived at the park and stayed there for more than an hour enjoying the exotic plants and the trees swarming with monkeys swinging about in complete freedom.

During the day it was sweltering hot and I dressed in a white shirt and shorts. The evenings were not quite so hot but the mosquitoes were out in force and to protect ourselves we wore long trousers and a long sleeved jacket.

At night I slept under a mosquito net but one night a cheeky blighter came in beside me and had a hearty meal before I managed to execute it.

For a few days I suffered from a mild attack of Prickly Heat. Talcum powder prevented it from worsening and then it slowly cleared. My sympathy went out to those who caught it very bad.

John and me went to the beach, the sand was lovely and soft just like that at Roker and we had it all to ourselves. I wondered why there were no people on it. Perhaps they hadn`t learned about beach recreation like us.

The waves were big but not rough, ideal for surfing. We fancied a swim but only a couple of yards out the water was very deep and we thought that sharks might swim in these waters. Maybe that is why people did not come but they could always sunbathe. We did. On second thoughts they are already brown.

Walking along the streets one evening it suddenly rained in torrents. No one ran for shelter they even came from inside and stood enjoying the cool refreshing rain pouring down on them, even us. It didn`t rain very long and when it had stopped we were soon dry.

When in the Market I bought a chatty and when we put out to sea I filled it with water and hung it outside of my porthole. The heat of the day made it sweat and the water inside was cooled and it came in handy when our water was rationed going to Malaya.

Over in Malaya the Japs had poisoned the local water supply so there was now an acute shortage of fresh water. For that reason local labour was engaged to clean all the available deep tanks at the bottom of the ship so that they could be filled with fresh water. In addition several huge vessels filled with fresh water were strapped to the deck. When fully laden we sailed for Port Swettenham in Malaya and our domestic water was rationed until we returned to India

PORT SWETTENHAM

Two days after leaving Madras we were at least 400miles from the Indian coast and now that the war was over the DEMs gunners began dumping dozens of cases of live ammunition into the sea. This operation continued until we were a similar distance from the Malayan coast then it was suspended.

Slowly the country we were to have invaded came into view. To reach the dock in Port Swettenham we had to sail up a long winding channel passing a number of small islands bristling with artillary and machine gun nests. I shudder to think what the outcome might have been had this invasion been for real.

Before the first merchantman was allowed to enter the port the Royal Navy gave the channel one quick sweep. It wasn't enough. We followed a French cruiser to the anchorage and both ships dropped anchor simultaneously. I was on deck at the time and I saw a huge column of water surge skyward which momentarily hid the Frenchie from my view.

A magnetic mine had exploded beneath the vessel and it settled in the shallow water. As soon as the anchor was slipped they must have switched off their de-gausing gear and allowed a magnetic mine to float up and strike the ship. Needless to say our de-gausing gear remained switched on until after we were safely tied up alongside. We then unloaded the water vessels which were on deck and proceded to pump the water from the deep tanks into containers on the shore.

With only a makeshift NAAFI, some military compounds and several longhouses there was little to interest us here in Port Swettenham. The length of a longhouse is about two hundred feet and there were many of these communal houses in this village. They were constructed without inside party walls. In their place curtains were hung. Each longhouse was occupied by several families.

I befriended a Malayan and he brought me to his room where I met his family. In this tiny space they had their meals and when they slept they drew the curtains together.

Walking along a street I heard merriment. People were letting off fireworks then they entered a longhouse singing and chanting emerging from the other end still singing. It was a Wake. A few days later I saw a wedding. No one was singing, no fireworks and no smiling faces.

About five miles inland was Klang a fair sized village which we visited several times. Here the shops were laden with all kinds of goods. The people were well clothed and did not look half starved which we had been led to believe. I formed the opnion that the population had not suffered under the Japanese occupation although those I spoke to claimed that they had. Unfortunately our conversations were in pigeon English and English. I was unable to purchase a phrase book so I was at their mercy. The evidence suggests that they lied and were just playing up to the new invaders. We called ourselves liberators. Before joining the MN I went to the cinemas back home and saw the news on the screen showing the North African campaign against the Italians in 1940. There was Sidi Barani, Mersa Matru, Bardia, Sollum, Tobruk and other small towns repeatedly changing hands and the local population waving flags bearing the Union Jack or the Italian Tricolor depending on who were marching in.

On the edge of this village were three big fields. In each was a similar brand of entertainment. They were called The Old World, The New World and The Happy World. There was an open air theatre where actors performed interesting Chinese plays.

The acting was very expressive making dialogue secondary. In addition there were sideshows, swings and round-a-bouts

We were warned against drinking the local brew as it was claimed that it affects the eyesight of Westerners only. We were easily led and became total abstainers except when on board we drank Australian lager.

Perhaps that was the reason for the warning.

Crossing the Bay of Bengal the dumping of ammunition was resumed.

On arriving in Calcutta I tried to contact my friends. They had moved on and we did not meet again until after we were all back in Civvy Street a few years after the end of the war.

We sometimes had a game of Tombola in a hall in Chowringee. It was operated in a big way. A game was played every half hour and the cost per card varied from 25annas to 100rupees. 100annas= 1rupee=one shilling and sixpence in old money, 7.5new pence The captain and chief steward were regular visitors and were luckier than us. Their luck held when they went to the racecourse.

This description is meant to help with the incident that follows

In the early months of the war when a ship was torpedoed any closed doors were jammed tight trapping seamen in their cabins being unable to escape through the small portholes. Eventually these were rectified in the older ships and became part of the design of new ships to be constructed.

Round portholes were now large enough to enable a big man to get through. Hinged at the top of the porthole was a round iron deadlight. This was supported by a chain from above enabling the glass window hinged at the side to open and close.

Slipping the chain allowed the deadlight to close over the glass so that light could not be seen from outside.

This is the incident.

It was so hot when we went ashore at night we left our portholes open. One night on our return we found dirty hands and footprints left by an intruder on the bed linen in one of our cabins. We discussed it and came up with a plan. The plan was put into action. A few nights went quietly by then it was my turn. The other engineers went ashore leaving their cabin lights on with the curtains closed. I lay on my bunk in the dark with the deadlight finally balanced by the chain. About an hour later I saw a brown arm snaking through the porthole and when it was well inside I let the chain slip from the deadlight. There was a howl of anguish and we had no more unsavoury visitors during the remainder of our stay.

We made another trip to Port Swettenham and I enjoyed my many excursions round the area. Until I came to sea I was conditioned to believe that we were the best and foreigners were useless and ignorant... I have had my eyes opened. One day I hitch hiked to Kuala Lumpur capital of Malaya. We travelled through jungle most of the way and on entering the city I marvelled at the architecture of the buildings. Even the railway station looked like a Sultans Palace. I was lucky to get a lift all the way back to the docks in an army jeep. Half way back and still in the jungle we had to stop while a ten foot snake crossed the road. Later I learned that terrorists had ambushed an army patrol on the same road I had travelled the previous day.

CALCUTTA AND THE RIOTS

On our return trip to Calcutta more cases of ammuniton were dumped. If other ships were disposing arms like us there will be a massive armoury in Davy Jones Locker now.

We berthed about a hundred yards from the Bathing Ghat where locals regularly bathed. One morning I had a perfect view of what appeared to be a religeous ritual which began very early and continued well into the evening.

There was a constant procession of men each man carrying an effigy of one of their gods or godesses and huge effigies resting on floats which were borne by small groups of men. On reaching the river they immersed themselves and their deities while chanting prayers. On leaving the river they made their way to their respective temples. This probably marked the start of the many riots which took place in the city during the remainder of our stay.

One night after this event John and me went to the Lighthouse cinema. Suddenly a riotous mob burst in ripping the seats from the floor and set the place on fire. The audience were terrified and panicked. We avoided the crowds and found a different way out of the burning building. Making our way back to the ship dodging rampaging gangs we saw the mounted police wading into the rioting mobs with their long iron bound bamboo poles (lathis) Other buildings were burning and I learned later that one of these was the Post Office.

This riot prevented us from going ashore again. Shore leave was cancelled. It didn't matter too much as we sailed two days later bound for Singapore.

SINGAPORE

The bulk of our cargo was made up with NAAFI stores. Secured to the deck were a few army vehicles. In addition we were to carry two passengers. They were REMI staff sergeants who in civilian life were engine fitters in one of the locomotive construction sheds in Leeds..They were quartered in the ships hospital and dined with us and we became good friends, We anchored off the island of Penang for a few hours to discharge some army supplies.

We arrived at Singapore docks in mid-morning and the two soldiers went ashore to report for duty at their base. They returned later in the day and asked the captain if they could stay on board until the ship sailed. He agreed so each day after breakfast they would go to their unit and return in time for tea and round the town with us.

While there I caught a slight touch of Malaria and an ear infection. I volunteered to do all the night duties for a week which would enable me to attend the Royal Naval Hospital. I took advantage of the situation to explore Singapore in the daytine.

Along the wharves lay dozens of Sampans. The aft end was covered by a canvas hood. This was the family home. They made a living by ferrying sailors to and from the warships and merchantmen lying at anchor in the bay. Depending on the time of day when coming aboard one would find members of the family either cooking or sleeping under the hood or perhaps fishing from the open part where the passengers sat.

Leaving the waterfront via the Elgin Bridge we passed a skyscraper which was known as The Cathay Building. Some of the upper floors were used by Lord Louis Mountbatten and his staff who controlled South East Asia Command, SEAC.

On the ground floor was a cinema screening shows of three hours duration commencing at 11-00am and the last performance starting at midnight.

In the town centre was Raffles Place boasting two clubs. The Shackles Club for service men and women and the very expensive Raffles Club.

There was a cemetery a short distance out of town. Here lay a grave with the body of an unknown soldier from the 1914-1918 war. It was well looked after.

Before we liberated Singapore Changi prison held allied prisoners of war. The role was now reversed. Allied soldiers now stood at the gates with Japanese prisoners inside. Outside some prisoners were sweeping the streets kow-towing to everyone wearing a uniform.

Singapore like Klang and Port Swettenham did not appear to have suffered under the Japs. The shops were well stocked but there was a shortage of cigarettes and soap which helped to create a flourishing black market. Motorised traffic was mainly confined to the military. Motor cars were conspicuous by their absence.

There was the conventional rickshaw pulled by a coolie and the more modern type hooked to a bicycle and pedalled by a coolie.

I was aproached by a local who asked me to smuggle drugs into India for him. It was well known that once involved in that traffic it was impossible to leave.

With my health problems behind me I was back on day work and was able to join the lads on their nightly jaunts.

We were invited to visit the aircraft carrier HMS Perseus lying at anchor in the bay. With us was about fifty more merchant seamen being ferried to the carrier.

Once on board we joined a number of RN sailors already standing on the flight deck. Slowly this section of deck was lowered to the deck below.

When in action this was the lift which moved aircraft in or out of the hanger.

A large area had been cleared and seats installed transforming it into the front stalls of a cinema. The film to be shown was "Alfs button afloat" starring Flanagen and Allen. After the show we were taken on a quick tour of the ship. To end the night we sampled the brews in some of the bars in town. There were no scare warnings here about drinking local ales

Our guests the two staff sergeants invited us to a dance which was to be held in the sergeants Mess on Boxing Night. We arrived at the barracks just after eight and found the party in full swing but where were the girls?. Beer was plentiful. I had not seen so much booze in one place all through the war years. There was a bowl of Punch continu ally being topped up and it wasn`t long before it took effect. No one noticed it at the time but we learned later it wasn`t just beer being used for topping up. I wonder what it was. A lot of horse-play went on, all in good fun. One soldier left the hall and returned carrying a NO GO signpost. When we left hours later the bowl was still full and so was I. Wending our way back to the ship through very smoky streets and alley-ways dimly lit by oil lamps under which sat groups of locals playing dice and smoking what smelled like opium. Unknowingly we had wandered into a no go area but encounted no trouble. The bars were still open, perhaps they never closed, but we had had quite sufficient for one night and we rolled our way back to the ship quite merry.

On New Years Eve we visited the NAAFI and various bars in town arriving back on board just before midnight just in time to join a party already in full swing in the second engineers room toasting the New Year in. We stood in a semi-cicle and Albert the host happened to fill Johns glass first then round the rest of the company and back to John.

Seeing his empty glass he promptly filled it up again. We raised our glasses and welcomed the New Year in where upon John flaked out. He was put to bed and he slept for twenty-four hours. After twelve hours we became a little anxious but the captain said "Dont worry" Sure enough after his resurrection he was himself again.

CHAPTER 6

1946 TO 1949

1946

We had intended to cross the island to see the causeway but as there was so much to see and do locally we never got around to it.

A big ship laden with NAAFI stores came in and tied up just ahead of us. Within minutes of the gangway being lowered several jeeps carrying redcaps (military police) arrived and took up positions along the whole length of the vessel. Some red caps went on board.

Looking ahead through my porthole I saw what appeared to be bottles and packages being thrown from several portholes. These were being salvaged by red caps in small boats. The captain and most of the crew were arrested for plundering the stores and were sent back to England. I never heard what the outcome was.

What I had been taught at school about the East was now being tested. Nothing better than being in the East and seeing it for yourself. I had been taught that poverty here was on a greater scale than at home but in India I had learned that much of it was due to the Caste System something to do with religion which prevented one from leaving the Caste they were born into.

I was watching men in an engineering shop doing work that I had been trained to do and I realised that the skills here were no less than ours back home. Our sailing orders came through. We were bound for the UK but we were to visit several ports on the way.

We made ready for sea and bade goodbye to the soldiers with whom we had had a great time.

COCHIN

The first was to be Cochin a small port in Goa on the south west coast of India which was at this time a Portuguese colony. On my previous voyage my cabin steward Louis was from this port.

We sailed through the Malacca Straits, rounded the island of Penang and set course due west into the calm Indian Ocean. The sun was beating down and it was very hot, hotter than in the engine room just like it was in Aden some time back. Skimming the water was a shoal of flying fish. Many tried to fly over the ship. Those that failed landed on the deck. These were collected and taken to the galley. Fresh fish was added to the menu.

We dropped anchor in the lagoon which was a natural harbour. The panoramic view was beautiful and wonderful for those interested in nature studies. There were no bars or impressive buildings. We stayed a few days loading cargo then sailed for Bombay.

BOMBAY

We berthed in the Blue Gate Dock. Every dock in Bombay was known by the colour of its gate. During our short stay every officer on board sampled the many exotic fruits which could not be bought in the UK. The mango was the most luscious and popular of them all and we were unable to stop eating them. We all paid the full price later. My memory of the taste and the after effects while crossing the Indian Ocean must be told.

Two days out of Bombay first one then another of all the Mates and Engineers went down with diarrhoea lasting at least three days. No man escaped the bug. In spite of being weak and listless no one missed a watch. Every officer stuck to his post but performed their duties mechanically. The weather was beautiful and those not on watch lay on deck in the sun or if feeling too ill took to their cabins. On the bridge the mates navigated as best as they could. They instructed the helmsman to steer a course due west in the hope that no ship would cross their path during the dark hours.

It was very hot in the engine room, the engineers wearing only shorts and shoes. Using the minimum of effort they struggled while attending to the main engine and auxiliary machinery.

A classic example of the current situation was when the fourth engineer on duty found himself in deep trouble. He phoned the chief for help who then sent me down to take over while the engineer relieved himself. I watched him climb the ladder and half way up he shouted "Too late" and the colour of his legs changed from a light tan to chocolate brown. When he returned to the floor plates I hosed him down then the ladders. I thought it prudent to start the bilge pump now rather than at the end of the watch. Three days later when the

First Mate returned to near normality he took a bearing and found that we were many miles off course. Maybe just as well being off the shipping lanes.

While hugging the Madagascar coast we were treated to an electric storm. It was moving at a slightly faster speed than we were so we had twelve hours of brilliant lightning flashes with Elmos Fire dancing along the arial wires between the two masts. Not one drop of rain fell.

Rounding the Cape of Good Hope on the way to Nigeria on the west coast of Africa I could see a smudge on the horizon I took to be Table Mountain.

LAGOS AND THE RIVER CONGO

Author with Tiger in Lagos 1946

After many days of pleasant sailing dropped anchor in the lagoon at the island city of Lagos. Opposite lay Appapa a small settlement built on the swampy mosquito infested mainland. Immediately I set foot on shore a little native boy maybe ten years old grabbed my arm and said that he wanted to be my friend. I tried to shake him off but he clung to me like a leech. I was surprised to hear speak in English. Later I learned that here on the coast only English was understood but not inland where they had their own language.

After vainly trying to get rid of him I relented and it turned out to be for the best. He called himself Tiger. Every time I came ashore he would be there waiting for me. As a guide he was perfect.

He took me into places in and beyond the city I would never had visited on my own or with an official tourist guide. I met some of his family and friends in their huts.

On Good Friday morning we sailed from Lagos and later anchored off the River Congo. Although the mouth of this river was thirty miles wide or more it was very shallow and we had to wait for the tide to rise before we could cross the bar and proceed upstream.

Meanwhile about twenty longboats each carrying about a dozen naked men and women all pulling at the oars were racing toward us. Each boat carried a river pilot. The overdressed pilot standing in the bow of the leading boat wore some sort of garment covered with ostrich feathers and sported a black silk top hat. When the boat came alongside he climbed up the Jacob ladder to the deck. In pigeon English he introduced himself as a river pilot and requested to guide us to Matadi seventy miles up the river and back. While he was discussing terms with the captain his retinue came aboard and the longboat was lifted out of the water and secured on deck.

On deck was a stack of empty oil drums waiting to be disposed of. The chief knew that the natives used oil drums to build shelters. He told us to chuck them over the side as this was an easy way to be rid of them. Balancing one of them on the bulwark we gestured to the natives then dropped it over the side. The race was on and the men and women in the boats nearest to the drum dived in and battled for possession.

After it had been won and put in the longboat we dropped another at the furthermost point from the boats and the race and battle for the drum was repeated. Each time a drum was dropped in the sea possession was heavily contested. We then decided to have some extra fun with the natives. The next drum was dropped aft and while this was being pursued another drum was taken right forward and a few holes were punched in it. Balancing it on the bulwark was the signal for another race. We waited until the boats were near then dropped it. There must have been a dozen bodies wrapped round the drum as it took in water and suddenly sank. When they came to the surface we pointed to more drums floating beside them, plenty for them all. Our last drum was placed amidships and when the boats gathered beneath it a pre-arranged signal was given and a flush of clean water gushed over the boats. It was all taken in good fun because when they were to return to shore every boat was stacked with empty oil drums and it hadn`t cost them a penny.

MATADI

The river mouth was now deep enough to cross the bar and we were under way again. For many miles we hugged the river bank which was covered in dense jungle. As the river narrowed we saw that the opposite bank was also covered by closely packed trees. At a right angled bend in the river about a mile before Matadi was a whirlpool we had to go through before continuing our journey upstream. This is where the pilot really earned his money. We were told that on many occasions some ships found themselves going back down the river after entering the whirlpool. I felt a weird sensation as the ship sailed through it but without any problems and we were soon tied up at the quay.

There is no twilight here and round about 6-00pm darkness falls swiftly and twelve hours later there is no dawn just sudden daylight. It was dark when we went ashore.

There were no lamps in the streets. The only light came from house windows and other buildings. It was almost as bad as the black out back home. Wandering through the town we came upon the Grand Hotel and we stayed there until it was time to return to the ship. Next day I watched a Mississippi type steamboat full of passengers going up river probably to Brassaville then John and me went ashore and made our way to the frontier only a couple of hundred yards away. We were in the Belgian Congo and on the other side was Angola a Portuguese colony.

On reaching the guard house we saw that it was unoccupied so we crossed no mans land to the Portuguese hut where we found the guards of both countries playing cards together. Using my improved French I told them where were from and were sightseeing and hoping to reach Noqui a couple of miles down the river. We were waved on. When we returned to Matadi we found the streets were absolutely empty. All shops and businesses were closed.

No one on the streets but us. It was mid-day with the sun at its hottest. For the locals it was siesta time. Only mad dogs and Englishmen go out in the mid-day sun.

I was given the next day off which was Easter Sunday but I was warned that the ship was moving to Noqui at 3-00pm.

No one would come with me on this jaunt so I went exploring alone.

Crossing the road from the dock gate I immediately entered into the thick jungle which covered half of the mountain I was now on. There were no trees on the top half and I can only guess that would be due to logging.

After a couple of hours climbing I reached the summit and before my eyes was a wonderful panoramic view of the area below me. Far down below was the MV Welsh Prince looking like a dinky toy set upon a white ribbon. I began my descent. About half way down I saw puffs of steam billowing from the funnel and a few seconds later I heard the faint blasts from the siren, a sign that it was preparing to sail. If it had gone without me it would only mean that I would have had to walk to Noqi only two miles away. As I went down I made for the railway track which went straight down to the dock.

Today being a holiday it was not being used so I went between the rails and sprinted between the sleepers. I was spotted racing down the track and as I came aboard the quartermaster gestured to the seamen to raise the gangway and we slowly moved away from the quay with our pilot to guide us once more through the whirlpool. An hour later we were safely tied up at a wharf in Noqi. We took on some more cargo and we sailed on Easter Monday morning. When we reached the estuary we had to wait again for the high tide because we now carried the maximum 2000tons of cargo allowed for us to pass over the bar. We hove to and lowered the longboat into the water then the pilot and his helpers followed. When the water was deep enough we sailed a few miles along the coast to Warri Creek then to Warri further inland. It was dark when a few hours later the mooring ropes were looped over the stumps of cut down trees which served as bollards. On the other side of the road opposite the dock gate was the jungle. The ships agent a black African was waiting for us and as soon as we had tied up he came aboard to meet the captain. He was dressed in the nineteenth century fashion wearing a black silk top hat, frock coat and tails.

He wore gum boots and was shaking his umbrella for it was raining in torrents turning the road into a deep muddy track. The following day the rain stopped and the sun quickly dried the mud on the road and after dinner I went into the jungle to explore. This time John Ellis came with me. No animals were to be seen but there were dozens of gaily coloured birds flying noisily around. After an hour or so we skirted a hill and came upon a lake where several women were bathing themselves and their children. When they saw us they appeared to be afraid probably because we were dressed like big game hunters wearing white shirt, shorts and toupee. They may have been thinking of the slave trade which was flourishing only a few years back and did not trust strangers.

I was told that even today they deliberately disfigured their children's faces hoping that this would deter slavers from taking their little ones. We waved to them as we passed but did not look back.

Leaving the jungle behind us we came upon the Welcome Inn. We bought a couple of beers and chatted with the bartender.

Business in the afternoon was very often slack as most people were at work but in the evenings it was very brisk. On our way back we chanced upon a dance hall and we looked in. What a sight to behold. The dancers appeared to be all Africans, the men were wearing frock coats and tails, the ladies in multicoloured print frocks and not one pair of shoes between them.

LAGOS AND MANCHESTER

We sailed next day for Lagos. When I went ashore there was Tiger at the gate waiting for me. He knew the exact time of our arrival and he remained my guide showing me more interesting places and meeting more of his associates until we sailed.

In port and at sea when it was warm it was common practice for engineers to wear only a singlet, shorts and shoes when on watch. After rinsing their sweaty underwear they would hang them on a rail to dry and leave their shoes on the engine room top grating, leave and go to their room to collect a towel and soap then go to the bathroom. After showering they returned to their room to dress.

For security reasons when in port all doors from the deck to the accommodation were locked and the only way in and out was by going through the bridge accommodation. There were no locks on the bathroom door.

We enjoyed good weather for the voyage from Lagos to Manchester. We sailed into the River Mersey Estuary then through the Manchester Ship Canal and arrived in Manchester 20th May seven days too early to qualify for the twelve months bonus.

The married deck and engineer officers sent for their wives to come and stay with them until the ship was due to sail. As in other ports normal security steps were followed but there were several brief encounters before the security arrangements were modified.

Before going home I called on my brother Bob a private in the Army Pay Corps and was billeted with the Tinkler family living in Moss Side Manchester. He was no longer the small evacuee I took to the railway station in 1939. After training with the army at Devises he had developed into a strong strapping youth and had added a few inches to his height.

I stayed on my ship for several days before leaving it for good and I returned home laden with carpets, fire side rugs, oriental bric-a-brac and happy memories.

At the end of my leave I was sent to Liverpool on relieving duties.

LIVERPOOL AND MV EMPIRE KENT

From Lime Street railway station I made my way down the very steep Lime Street to the River Mersey. Along the riverside were several docks along which ran the overhead railway. There was a station at every dock entrance and the MV Empire Kent was in the Canada Dock in Bootle and I was to relieve one of its engineers for a short while

This was a ship taken from the Germans to partly compensate the companys shipping losses suffered during the war. The main machinery was a M.A.N. diesel engine, all information was in German.

Hanging on a wall in the smoke room was an interesting painting. It showed the final move in a chess game with one king in check-mate.

The losing group of surviving pieces wore hangdog expressions. The faces of the victorious chess men were covered in broad smiles. I saw this as a caricature of the war between the Allies and the Axis Powers. I don't think the painter had the same idea as me.

In a nearby dock was the MV Malayan Prince the ship my friend Davy Robson had first sailed on in 1940. Some months later he transferred to the MV Siamese Prince which when homeward bound was torpedoed and sunk off the Irish coast and he was lost. I visited this ship and met the engineers, some were ex-work mates from Doxford.

In a Bootle pub after telling a girl I was from the north-east she insisted that I was Welsh just because I could pronounce Aberystwyth correctly. At the end of the night she still did not believe me. The short time that I was here I was still able to go home for the week-end and my only disappointment was that we never put to sea.

On Friday my last day here the superintendent instructed me to go home for the week-end and on Monday go to Hull to sign on the SS Samdaring.

MV JAVANESE PRINCE

I caught the afternoon train arriving home in the evening to find a telegram waiting there for me. "Do not go to Hull. SS Samdaring engineer decides to remain with ship. Instead proceed to Swansea and report to the chief engineer on the MV Javanese Prince for relieving duties".

I left home early Monday morning for a train to Swansea. On this train I met a senior engineer who was going to join the same ship. We arrived in Swansea late evening and he suggested we book into a hotel for the night as it would be difficult to find the ship in the dark. We had a meal then turned in. Next morning we found the vessel by 9-00am. I met the engineers and one was John Rumph who had served his time at Doxfords with me. I learned later that I knew the wife of the second engineer. She was a hairdresser in a shop close to my home where I went to have my hair cut. She had a half brother Bill Burnside who had worked with me at Doxfords. Bill was also a volunteer at the Colliery School FAP.

Her husband Mr Schofield who I had just met progressed to be the engineering superintendent for the Prince Line visiting vessels of the line in ports all over the UK. Unfortunately a few years later he was killed in a train crash. The Javanese Prince was fitted with a six cylinder Doxford engine, three diesel generators each one was as big as the main engine I was used to. In port these generators were looked after by shore fitters. One day a connecting rod crashed through the casing causing a lot of damage. I couldn`t understand why we didn`t look after them.

While here in Swansea I went looking for my old haunts. Sadly the ATS camp and the NAAFI were both boarded up. The war was over. The Patti Pavilion was still functioning but the magic was missing. I looked in the Billiard Hall to see if the girl I had once dated was still around. She was not.

I signed Articles and we sailed on 7th December and a few hours later we were in a Liverpool dock.

By chance my cousin Harry Wharton also a marine engineer happened to be here in Liverpool and we bumped into each other in the town centre. He had a cousin Beatty Wharton whom I had known in our childhood days.

She was now married to a German ex-prisoner of war and now living in Birkenhead. Harry suggested that we visit them. We were made very welcome and we talked of our childhood days. My knowledge of German was very limited but he having been in England for several years understood our language. We got on well together and I told him of the school camp at Hexham when we had a German student with us in 1935. I believe this meeting may have been the beginning of a long process towards softening my attitude toward the German people.

I was in Liverpool over Xmas and New Year spending most of my time in the pubs which I thought were rather quaint. Drinks were served in the passage ways as well as in the bar and rooms

Nine members of the MV African Prince having been with her for two years were to be relieved and a few days after New Year I was sent home on standby and to be ready to leave home at short notice to join her in New York. Final instructions for my departure would be sent by telegram. Little did I know then that my next voyage was to be my last.

1947

January was an extremely cold month with regular snow showers. The bad weather worsened and the snow covered roads badly affected transport.. Coal deliveries were running very late leaving many households including ours short or without coal. During the next few days I cycled to Roker beach to collect sea coal. As the tide receded it left the sea coal among the pebbles and I had to be careful when filling the bag.

The coal blackened the pebbles and I had to be careful selecting the coal. Any pebble finding its way on a fire exploded when hot and whizzed across the room. It took me a long time to fill a bag as scores of people were doing the same. Putting the bag of coal on the bike I pushed it home. Learning that coal was being washed up on Hendon beach I went there for my next few bags.

The Colliery School FAP. and all the other ARP establishments had closed down long ago. On Saturday night I went to the Rink wearing civilian clothes. There I met some of my old friends from the Dancing School, The Alex and the Rink. They were Billy Richardson, Betty Watson, Nancy Wake and several more. They told me they were all going to the Clarion Cycling Club dance at Wetheralls on Tuesday night and I agreed to meet them there.

MEETING RUTH

Ruth in WAAF's 1942

On entering Wetheralls Dance Hall wearing my MN badge in the lapel of my civilian clothes I looked across the hall and saw this girl standing at the bandstand and our eyes locked for a few seconds but it felt like an eternity. The band played and dancers came between us and broke the spell. I saw my friends and I joined them. I danced with Nancy Wake, Renee Watts and Mary Booth and each time I came near that girl a strange feeling came over me and at first avoided looking at her.

I had never experienced this sensation before and it bothered me. I intended to find out why so I decided to have the next dance with her. It was a modern waltz and I made my way toward her. I have been refused in the past but that was no reason why my courage failed me now and I asked her friend instead. With her I returned to my normal self and we chatted and exchanged names. Her name was Jean Conlin.

When I escorted her back to her seat she introduced me to Ruth. I sensed that this meeting was different to my previous escapades and I fought against it mainly because in a few days time I expect to be away for two years. This hadn't bothered me in the past. Why now?. For the rest of the evening I shared dances with Ruth, Jean and Nancy. I felt as if I had known Ruth all my life and I had only met her an hour ago. It was very disturbing and I wasn't too sure how to cope. In attempt to be off-handed I told that I had come to the end of my leave and expect to be away by the week-end and not return home for two years. In reply she said "Come and have a cup of tea and let us enjoy ourselves now and let the future look after itself".

In the conversation that followed I learned that she had served nearly five years in the WAAFs. I had the last dance with Ruth. It was 1-00am and snowing hard when I left the hall with Ruth and Jean and there was a thick covering on the ground. I walked with them to the top of Silksworth Row bank. Conditions were so bad we did not linger to talk. As I moved to leave them Ruths parting words were "We come to Wetheralls every Saturday and if you are still at home why not come along". I reminded her that I expect to receive the telegram on Monday and be away long before Saturday. We then set off for our respective homes. They were going to Ford Estate and I was going in the opposite direction to Monkwearmouth.

Saturday arrived but not the telegram. Should I go to Wetheralls?. I wanted to meet Ruth again but I was afraid of the consequences. I have already had an extra week at home. Surely I cannot expect another. All day I wondered what I should do.

In the past I had never worried whether I kept a date or not. I hadn't arranged a meeting with her so why was I worrying now?. I kept putting off until it was nearly too late to go. The band was playing the medley when I arrived at the door and I asked the doorman to tell Ruth that I was here. Arriving so late I did not even expect her to come out but she did.

She told me that she had thought that I must be away and was pleased that I had come even at this late hour. The expression on her face told me that she really was pleased to see me. She went back into the hall to tell Jean that she was going to walk home with me. Jean could catch a bus. We walked slowly and on the way I explained that I was still waiting for the telegram and that time must now be very short.

We agreed to meet next day in the town and it was fine and dry. We boarded a tram which took us to Grangetown. From there we walked along the cliff tops to Ryhope and back. We parted in the town centre. Arranging another meeting she explained that every Monday she attended Holy Communion classes and Conformation being so close she couldn`t afford to miss one but would like to meet me on Tuesday if that was all right.

It snowed all day and it was bitterly cold when we met so we went in the Ritz cinema where it was warmer. On Wednesday night the ground was covered with snow but it was fine and not so cold.

From the Round Robin Pub, Ruths home was only a five minutes walk away, we walked to the South Hylton riverside and back and I caught the last bus to the Wheat Sheaf. Two minutes later I was home

On Thursday night the weather was atrocious, the snow was pelting down. We had arranged to go to a private dance in the Bay Hotel on the sea front at Seaburn. It was to go on till 1-30am and a special bus was engaged to take the dancers home.

Seeing no improvement in the weather we left earlier to make sure that both of us were able to get home using the normal bus services. I left Ruth at her gate and then I caught the last bus to the Wheat Sheaf.

On Friday morning the telegram arrived for me to go London for final instructions to join the MV African Prince in New York. It was a fine dry night when we met for the last time before starting on my long journey. I gave Ruth the telegram to read. She said that it had to come and we had to come to terms with it. We discussed how a separation of two years could affect us and decided to write only as friends and one was to inform the other immediately if either wished to sever our relationship. We also made pact "No secrets, no lies" I did not realise it at the time but this pact was the means of cementing us together for forty-five good happy years. There were some thorns and weeds in our bed of roses but we learned how to prevent them from choking the flowers. We parted and I went home to prepare myself for the long journey ahead.

The month of January had been very cold with a lot of snow but the first of February was the real start of the most severe and atrocious winter in the UK for many years which I was to miss. I was pleased that I had left a reasonable supply of coal at home.

Early that morning I went to London by train. I called at the Prince Line office for final instructions where I was introduced to two engineers John Mars from Glasgow and Jackie Atkinson from Philadelphia near Sunderland and nine ratings from various parts of the UK. Holding the highest rank I was given all the travel documents to look after. After completing the formalities we had about three hours to spare so we three engineers went to a cinema. An hour later there was a power cut.

We waited half an hour in vain for the show to re-start so we left the cinema and made our way to the railway station and boarded the boat-train.

RMS AQUITANIA

It took us alongside the RMS Aquitania at the Southampton Dock quayside. The snow began to fall as we climbed the gangway which led into the side of the liner. Going in was like entering the foyer of a four stars Grand Hotel. Facing me were two huge sweeping staircases. One to the left, the other to the right. Seating was inadequate for so many passengers. All the seats and settees on this deck were occupied and hundreds more passengers were to arrive after us. We engineers travelled first class, the nine seamen were on the second class deck. I never saw them again until the ship docked in Halifax. This was my second experience as a passenger and I enjoyed every minute of the voyage. Next morning Sunday we began the voyage to Halifax Nova Scotia leaving behind a very bad winter which was to become much worse before February and March were out.

The next few weeks must have been desperate for all at home. I only hoped that the few bags of sea coal I had left would last out until the proper coal was delivered.

We heard over the ships radio that after we had sailed an unexploded bomb was found in the dock where we had been tied up.

On board were families going to America and Canada to start a new life. GI brides to join their American husbands. American and Canadian men and women returning home from war service. A real mixed bag of people.

Sharing a dining table with us three were Flight Officer S Hurdle from Wynyard Saskatchewan. T Day from Long Sound Ontario both in the RCAF.

P Minster a Dutch Army Officer from Fluiskill Holland and Canadian Nursing Division nurses Margaret Walls and Rita Watkins from Hamilton Ontario.

We often played table tennis with other passengers. One of the best I played against was sixteen years old Barbara Lovett daughter of a couple bound for Vancouver. She turned out to be an accomplished piano accordion player and was one of the volunteer artists to perform on the ships concert on our last night at sea.

Being mid-winter I had expected a rough passage. The crossing was pleasant with only a moderate swell which barely affected the liner as it was fitted with stabilisers.

It was still uncomfortable for a few passengers as someone on the deck above left their cabin to puke over the side and I was unfortunate to be directly below and for a while I did not smell very nice.

We arrived in Halifax on Friday morning and there on the railway tracks next to the quay were six very long trains waiting to pick up passengers from the liner. Each train would be pulled by two massive steam locomotives. Their destinations were to all parts of the USA and Canada. Ours was to terminate in New York.

Immigration officers came on board and made an announcement over the tannoy system. All passengers on hearing their names called were to attend the immigration desk for clearance. Our hopes of a sight seeing tour of Halifax were dashed as our party was among the last to be called

HALIFAX TO NEW YORK

Our train left at midnight and I stood at a corridor window looking on to the snow covered landscape illuminated by the lights shining from the carriages.

After a very short time there was nothing to be seen but snow. Not a building, not a tree or bush. It was an empty wilderness so I retired to my reserved compartment, pulled the bed down from the wall and was soon fast asleep. It was daylight when I woke up. I was barely ready when a steward knocked on my door and told me breakfast was being served. All that could be seen outside was a huge expanse of open country covered with a mantle of snow. For a long time the train ran parallel to the River Lawrence and its many islands. A couple of hours after leaving the river the train made its first stop at a station seemingly in the middle of nowhere. I saw only a few scattered trees on the snow covered prairie and a horse drawn carriage standing by waiting to pick up some passengers from the train.

Looking closely at the horizon I saw a smudge and I was told that it was Newcastle where those people climbing into the taxi were going.

Our next stop was in the main street of Monkton. It was strange to see two big engines coupled to a long string of carriages standing on a thoroughfare in the middle of town. Close by was a post office and us three went in and bought view cards to send home. I was still writing when I heard the whistle from the train. Leaving the stamped cards on the table we ran after the train and jumped aboard just like a clip from the wild west movies. The cards were not delivered.

Approaching Montreal very late in the evening the train ran full pelt into a snow drift burying both engines and the first five carriages. Our carriage was a long way back.

It took eight hours to clear the tracks and we took advantage of the delay to see a little of Montreal and talk to some of the people. We did not meet one Canadian born person. They were newcomers from Scotland and France. The tracks are now cleared.

Coming to the Canadian/ US border we were advised by the steward to buy our meals while still in Canada as once over the border prices are doubled.

Travelling for sixty hours from leaving Halifax we passed through Monkton, Montreal, Vermont, Springfield arriving in New York Central Station at midday on Monday. If we had come to Halifax a few weeks later we would have travelled to New York by ferryboat taking twelve hours.

NEW YORK

Three taxis took our squad to the Times Square Hotel where we were to stay until the arrival of the MV African Prince. We three engineers were each given a well furnished room with a telephone, radio and television. None of us had any idea how to operate the television so it remained a mystery to me for a considerable length of time.

In one of the many Mayflower restaurants in the city we spent more than ten minutes discussing what to have. Jackie of slight build became a little ruffled and Jock a big lad picked him up and sat him on top of a radiator and told him to stay there until he had cooled down.

After our meal we went sightseeing along Broadway, Fifth Avenue and forty-second Street. Looking in a shop window I saw TVs for sale. On one I saw a diver on the sea bed examining a wrecked ship.

Nearly every building had a large brilliantly lit advertising sign on its front. One of them was advertising Camel cigarettes and showed the image of a man smoking with little puffs of smoke coming from his mouth.

The cinemas, theatres, Western Union, bars, cabarets, night clubs cafes, pool rooms, drug stores, department stores, shops, restaurants and hamburger stalls were open for business day and night. A boon for shift workers who were able to enjoy social life at any time. However all businesses must close at any time for at least one hour for cleaning. Most bars closed at 5-00am or 6-00am. Even at 3-00am the sidewalks were heaving with people. We returned to the hotel at 3-00am and turned in.

While here in the Times Square Hotel Jackie wrote a letter to his uncle who was currently working in a gold mine somewhere in Brasils interior and informed him that we were to go to Santos shortly.

On our return to New York a letter from his uncle was waiting for Jackie. His uncle had arranged to have two weeks off work and from the expected day of the ships arrival he would stand outside of the Furness Withy Office between 8-00pm and 9-00pm,

On our second morning the companys agent called at the hotel and gave us a few dollars. This time he advised us to have dinner then go to Pier 80 and await the arrival of the MV African Prince now due. It was not unusual for British ships to trade in foreign waters for five years or more without returning to the UK. In such a case the crew having served two years were relieved and sent home.

MV AFRICAN PRINCE

The MV African Prince and the MV Tudor Prince were two such vessels on the New York to Buenos Aires trade route calling at various ports in between. There were times when the two ships would dock in the same port and the crews would have fun together.

Of the six serving engineers three of them will be preparing to leave when the ship docks. The turn of the other three will be in March.

She arrived late in the afternoon and when safely tied up alongside and the gangway lowered three engineers and nine seamen came ashore carrying their belongings. After a brief greeting and farewell we went aboard and changed into working gear. Half an hour later we sailed bound for Boston. On this run I thought back on those few days I had with Ruth and wondered if we would meet again.

BOSTON

When we arrived in Boston I received the first of many letters from Ruth and with each came a settling thought that we would meet again but my confused thoughts urged me to carry on as I had always done, ce sera sera.

It was cold but unlike in New York there was no snow on the ground. Jock was on night watch so only Jackie and me wandering through town came upon the Imperial Bar which in style was different to those back home.

In the interior were cubicles with low partitions very much like those in an ice cream parlour. On entering we passed by a stage on which a dance band dressed as cowboys were playing the latest hit songs, Always, Deep in the heart of Texas, Give me five minutes more of your charms and others. At the far end was the service bar and in between were the rows of cubicles. On the table was a radio, the volume tuned loud enough for the occupants to hear but not enough to disturb others. We collected our drinks and sat in an empty cubicle. We had only been sat down a few minutes when a US Coastguard and his girl friend entered and sat opposite. They were both very, very drunk.

They started to converse with us and soon the girl became suggestive and the sailor became angry with her and heated words were exchanged. After a while they cooled down but soon the girl carried on as before and of course we played along with her enjoying the banter. The sailor left the cubicle for drinks as we thought. But no. Two women in the next cubicle having heard the whole episode leaned over and told us that they knew this coastguard and that he was a trouble maker and he would return not with drinks but with pals to take us on and suggested that we should leave.

Outside they inroduced themselves as Mrs Swallow and daughter Caroline. They were very nice to talk with and they invited us to come with them to their home and meet the rest of the family. It was after midnight when we arrived. It was a very big house and all the lights were out. Everyone had gone to bed. This was Boston not New York. After settling down with a drink she went upstairs and roused the household saying that they had been invaded by the English. Within minutes three scantily dressed females came into the room and we were introduced to them. We talked of the air raids at home, life on the high seas and post war life at home and still on rations. They spoke of how we came to be with them and of life in general here in Boston. It was almost dawn when we left promising to call on our next visit to Boston. We sailed next day for New York and never ever returned to Boston.

NEW YORK

On our return to New York a letter from his uncle was waiting for Jackie. His uncle had arranged to have two weeks off work and from the expected day of the ships arrival he would stand outside of the Furness Withy Office between 8-00pm and 9-00pm,

This time we were in New York for a little over two weeks. Two engineers arrived to take over the duties of those ready to go home. The third engineer well past forty did not wish to be relieved and so remained. The other five were all under thirty years old and with the third engineer staying he done us all a favour. When in port four of us had to take turns at keeping a watch aboard and the third engineer often volunteered to take these over enabling us to have more time ashore. For that we were all grateful.

The British Merchant Navy Club was on the top floor in the Astor Hotel and we visited it several times during our stay. Dances were held there every night and the hostesses were very friendly. There was one girl from Staten Island who kept me right with the American language. I had told her that I thought that she was very homely and she explained that here the expression was insulting quite the opposite meaning that we have.

Ruths current favourite tune was "Symphony" and I asked Mrs Muir the pianist to play it for me and she did every time I came. I would just sit and listen to it being played and thinking of Ruth and what may be. Yes it was affecting me but I still tried to carry on as if she was just another girl. I explored most of Manhatten all the way from Harlem to down town where the streets were laid out in an English haphazard way. They were probably built by the earlier settlers before the numbered avenues and streets were laid in an orderly way such as Broadway, 5th Avenue and 42nd Street and the rest in Manhatten.

The weather here was very bad. Even after the snow ploughs had done their work the roads were still covered in snow and the pavements were piled high with the snow shovelled from the roads. The bad conditions did not appear to interrupt the traffic very much. Everything was in full swing.

We walked along 92nd Street in Harlem the Negro quarter and then down to Broadway stopping at Jack Dempseys restaurant and bar. We met and chatted with Jack Dempsey the ex-champion heavy weight boxer of the world.

Another day saw us in the Empire Sate Building. We entered a lift which took us to the 50th floor then changed to a second to take us up to the 102nd floor. From there we climbed stairs to reach the Observation Tower. We were told that on a clear day one could see over a distance of eighty miles. Today I could only see half of that distance. While on the tower we befriended an American and had a photo taken of us.

There was a studio where I recordered an audio letter on a cardboard disc which was sent on to my parents for them to play on the gramophone.

Jackie and me were given complimentary tickets to attend a radio show in Radio City Studio on 5th Avenue. It was a canny show but it was rigged. Before it commenced the audience was told how to respond to the various acts. In one of the wings a man would raise a large card with instructions telling us when to applaud, cheer, boo, clap hands, jeer or stamp your feet.

We sailed from New York and soon we were in Philadelphia and were loaded up with about a hundred motor cars. We were here only two days and as I was duty engineer on the first night I saw very little of the Town before sailing for Chester.

CHESTER

It was mid-morning when we docked in Chester. One of the pistons was due to be de-carbonised and work on it was to be started as soon as "Finished with engines" was rang. All the parts needed to reach the piston were removed and we began to lift the piston from the cylinder. At this stage we received an order to move to another berth immediately. It all had to be put together then we moved to the allotted place and began stripping the parts down again. Once again we were as far on as before ready to raise the piston when believe it or not we were informed that we were in the wrong place and the port authorities insisted that we moved. At mid-night after a trying day the job was finished but the ship was not moved.

We three dashed to the showers, cleaned up and slipped ashore before another silly order came through. We tried a couple of bars and then at 3-00am found us in Woolworths chatting the shop girls up.

There were very few people around. Except for the shops this is more like our English towns where most people slept through the night. After a couple of hours kip we were on duty manoeuvring the ship into the dry dock where we ought to have been in the first place. All the skin fittings were to be examined and the propeller was to be replaced.

During this very cold weather the 3rd engineer done his own night watch aboard and did not volunteer to do any of ours. It fell to me to supervise the changing of the propellers which began at 7-00pm. when the shore fitters came on board.

It snowed all night and it was fourteen degrees Fah. below zero. The working area at the stern was surrounded by braziers burning coke to warm the propeller and shaft to help ease the removal of the old propeller and fitting the new one on. The job was completed by 6-00am. I went along for breakfast and then at 7-00am started on my normal work and in the evening went ashore with the lads.

Knowing that we were going to Brasil I bought a Portuguese/English phrase book so that I could learn about forty every day phrases to help to find my way around Santos.

On the voyage down the third engineer saw me studying this phrase book and he gave me a "Teach yourself Portuguese" book to help me along.

As we sailed from Chester the wind was howling and snowing heavily with the seas crashing over the bow ceaselessly. Heading south into tropical waters the weather slowly improved until it was so calm the ships wake stretched to the horizon unbroken.

CROSSSING THE LINE

Author captured 1947

Author in King Neptune's court 1947

Approaching the equator an old time custom was exercised. The only men not taking part in the ritual of crossing the line (equator) were the watch keepers. The older men volunteered to take over all watch keeping duties. Those who had been through this ritual before took on the roles of King Neptune, the Queen, Court Prosecutor, Barber, Secret Police and Nymphs. The rest which included me were to go into hiding. For safety reasons the bridge, all accommodations and engine room were put out of bounds. On being found by the secret police the victim was brought before the court and charged on some offence, tried and of course found guilty.

I was found and dragged from my hiding place and taken to court where I pleaded not guilty having crossed the line twice a few months back on the way from Singapore to Lagos via the Cape when I was an engineer on the MV Welsh Prince.

Unable to produce evidence I was found guilty and duly sentenced. I was lathered with a mixture of oil, sawdust and washing up liquid and shaved by the Barber. The Nymphs then helped to dump me in a tank fashioned from a tarpaulin sheet filled with sea water. After the last victim had been punished we all turned on our captors untill all were in the tank and a good time was had by all. I was presented with a certificate signed by King Neptune and Captain Martin to prove that I had crossed the line.

SANTOS

After a couple of weeks at sea we dropped anchor in Santos Bay.

Brazil was a coffee producing country and within days tea and cocoa were replaced by coffee which was served by the pint seven times every day until we reached London several weeks later.

We were here for eight weeks and I had some wonderful experiences. The first two nights we remained at anchor in the bay. A liberty boat plied between all of the ships at anchor and the shore near the Casablanca Bar every hour. On leaving the liberty boat we three went into the Casablanca bar and I chatted with the barmaids in their lingo practising my forty phrases. Seated at the next table was a group of Norwegians already well oiled. We conversed with them, their English was quite good but before long their mood changed and made derogatory remarks so we left them and went to Roberts Bar close by which was to become our local.

When it was nearly 8-00pm we went to the Furness Withy office hoping to meet Jackies uncle. His uncle had not turned up by 9-00pm so we went on a crawl. Being Good Friday many colourful religious processions paraded the streets all evening. We watched them as we meandered between the bars.

We returned to the quay and went in the Casablanca to wait for the last ferry. The last boat leaves the shore at midnight resulting in the area being packed with seamen many the worse with drink.

Our hostile Norwegian friends were already there already well and truly plastered. We sat away from them but they saw us and continued where they had left off.

We we went over to them and asked them to lay off but they just laughed and made more rude remarks. Jock picked up a beer barrel and dropped it on the lap of one of them and all three got stuck in. Within a few seconds there was pandemonium and there was a real set to with the rest of the seamen joining in. I don`t think they knew who they were fighting or why. The police arrived wading in with their batons. The barmaids with whom we had been chatting with earlier came and dragged us into a room behind the bar. We never saw the Norwegians again even though we visited this bar a few times before sailing.

Next day being Easter Saturday Ruth was to be confirmed by Alwyn Williams the Bishop of Durham in the Church of the Good Shepherd and I wondered what she would think of my behaviour the previous night. Then I said to myself "What does it matter? I am away for two years and anything can happen in that time" so I dismissed the thought.

The ship left the anchorage and came alongside. We were now able to go ashore and in the evening we went to the office again and imagine Jackies delight when he saw his uncle standing there. To reach us he had travelled 1,000miles by plane to Rio de Janeiro then 200miles by train to Santos.

We went the rounds with him and a few more times in the two weeks that he was here. and on his last night we had a farewell party on board for him.

It was Easter Monday and I was given the day off and I went out to explore the town. I stood outside of a magnificent building. Being curious I climbed the steps and went inside the foyer. It was a bank. I was wearing clothes unlike those worn by the locals and an armed guard came over to me and asked what I wanted.

Of course I couldn`t understand him. I showed him my phrase book and using the little bit of the language I knew I explained that I was an English sailor looking round the town. This encounter resulted in him inviting me to his home that evening. I returned to the bank to meet him at the end of his shift. He took me to his home and introduced me to his wife Maria.

His name was Maurice. They were both about my age. In the seven remaining weeks of my stay in Santos I visited them three times a week and learned to converse with them fairly easily in their language. I brought Jackie along a couple of times and tried to teach him some phrases but he packed up and gave up trying. I also practised on the dockers discharging the cargo. One of them was Carlos and he took me to the campus where he lived and I met some of his friends. One day I invited him to a meal on board and as he knew no English I had to interpret for him and then to my fellow officers.

On Sunday nights I attended the Baptist Church. Being a foreigner and able to talk with them I was of some interest. There were some snags at times. I was telling them about Ruth and one of the girls thought I was talking about her and I was trying to date her. I managed to ward off her amorous attention without any complications.

We came to know the staff in Roberts Bar and I learned a lot about them. They worked here because in their own little village there was no work for them. After working here a month they went home for a few days. They knew some English so it was easier for Jock and Jackie to mix in.

Some days later the MV Tudor Prince tied up alongside and one of its engineers came aboard looking for old shipmates. They were the engineers we had relieved in New York. About half a dozen of us sat with him in the 2nd eng. room chatting and drinking for two hours. Our visitor would only drink lemonade while telling us of an experience he did not like. On a previous visit he was in trouble with the police by being drunk and disorderly. He didn`t want a repeat performance.

We all went ashore linking arms with our new friend in the middle. Rolling along from side to side singing our heads off heading for Roberts Bar we were stopped by two armed policemen and they took our friend away. They had known that his ship was in port and they had recognised him and wrongly assumed his condition because of us. A short time later they returned him to us in Roberts Bar. At the end of the night the police may have been justified in taking us all in including the one who disliked their lock-up but we all returned safe and sound.

I had a full Sunday off so I took the opportunity to go to Sao Paula a new city in the making on a plateau 3,000ft above sea level. The bus left Santos and began the long climb up the torturous winding road to the city. Driving at the right side of the road meant that the bus was close to the mountain`s side. It was also daylight and the hazards went by unnoticed by me.

Walking through the sunlit broad streets with skyscrapers nearly as high as those in New York was most impressive and I found it hard to believe that in Brasil's interior there were people living under stone age conditions.

It was night time and from the road I looked down and saw the lights of Santos far below. The return journey was frightening.

Going down this mountain road on the right brought the bus to the edge overlooking a sheer drop to the sea and no crash barriers at the roadside and I thought it most alarming that traffic used this road every day.

An Argentinean vessel lay alongside and we had a friendly game of football against its crew on the quayside. There was no referee and a number of doubtful goals were scored.

During the unloading an incident happened which highlighted the dangers that were ever present. A car being winched from the hold was intended to be swung over to be lowered to the quay. This one crashed on the ships bulwark and folded like book.

Part of the next cargo to be loaded were bananas bound for a boot polish factory in Buenos Aires Argentina.

If I had remained here I would have become very fluent. In fact after I was married to Ruth we both considered emigrating to Brasil. At the time there were great opportunities here for the likes of me like Jackies uncle who was doing very well.

I bade farewell to Maurice and Maria fully expecting to meet up with them again after a few weeks.

Leaving the hot climate behind we sailed south bound for Buenos Aires. As we came nearer to our destination it became very cool. It was winter.

BUENOS AIRES

At this time Buenos Aires had the reputation of being the cleanest city in the world. For me it lost that distinction when we arrived. The city was in the grip of a dustbin strike. Garbage was piled high everywhere. We were here long enough after the strike to see the city regain its reputation.

A young seaman from the previous voyage never left the ship in the six weeks we were here. Waiting at the dock gate was a young girl who asked everyone leaving the ship if this seaman was on board. He had implored all on board to tell her that he had gone home. She was still at the dock gate waiting when we sailed away.

Many of the bars were very near to the docks. One group was well known as "Underneath the Arches" two of them were the Bristol and the Derby. Nearby was the Paris Dancing. In the city centre was La Nidito and along the riverside in Lavalle was the La Maisonette Russe all in easy walking distance from the dock. It was a thirty minutes bus ride to Nicks Bar.

On our first night we went ashore with several chaps from the original crew and as soon as we stepped inside of the Derby Bar a barmaid picked up the phone and I heard her say "African Prince". Within minutes a couple of armed policemen came in but soon left. I think this crowd was kept under surveillance for the night. Here drinks were sold by the glass. They were smaller than half a pint.

The chief, Jackie and myself left the Derby to visit the Paris Dancing which translated into English means Dance Hall. No sooner had we sat at a table than a bevy of girls sat beside us. We ordered beers for us, whisky for the ladies. The whisky was actually cold tea and these girls were working so had to remain sober.

We were aware of this practice. Their English was very poor and conversation was difficult.

One of them with a terrible mixture of Spanish and English said how cold it was. The others hadn`t a clue what she had said so I tried my Portuguese, no good then I tried my schoolboy French and it worked. This girl had also learned French at school. This is what I asked her "Vous portons les panterlons laineux n`est pas" Her unexpected reply was "Non, je le ne porte pas rien" I didn`t believe her so I asked her "Vous leverons la jupe s`il vous plait" and she did and I saw that she had spoken the truth. My few phrases had once again come in handy. We left for the La Nidito in the city centre where I met Helen. I made a date to meet her on the next night.

About a half dozen of the lads came to the rendezvous with me and when she arrived they bundled her into a taxi bound for I don`t know where to. They said it was for my own good. We then went to La Masonette Russe in La Fayette.

It was furnished in what I thought to be a Russian style with carpets, drapes, table cloths all coloured red. Even the lamp shades were radiating a soft red glow. The bandsmen were dressed as Cossacks wearing fine embroided white silk shirts playing music, mostly Russian on balalaikas, lutes and piano accordions. They played D`Attendrai, Always and Black eyes but they did not know Symphony.

Another night this time on my own I called in the Derby and in Spanish asked for a beer. A phrase everyone knew. A chap standing beside me asked a question in Spanish. Not able to buy a phrase book I didn`t know what he had said to me so I answered him in Portuguese and surprisingly he understood.

He was from Chile and was an engineer on the SS Arica which by chance was moored beside my ship. We talked in Portuguese with a little bit of Spanish from him and a little bit of English from me. We got on well together and on the way back to the dock he invited me aboard his vessel for a curry and to meet his shipmates.

Not knowing a lot about curry I ate the chilli that was with it. My mouth was on fire. They thought it was a huge joke. I spoke Portuguese all the others spoke Spanish and my new friend was our interpreter. It was an interesting debate. They sailed next day.

I caught a collectivo, similar to a mini bus a thirty minute ride along the riverside road. to take me to Nicks Bar. The violinist and pianist were a mother and daughter duo. I asked them to play Symphony and they did. Every time I visited this bar they played it for me..

Here I met a Russian seaman and was able to speak with him using French. He was a political exile unable to return to Russia.

The wet docks here were unique. From a book I learned that they were built on reclaimed land. The docks were parallel to each other and the land spaces between the sheds at each dock were landscaped with trees, bushes, grass and flowers and people came here for a Sunday morning walk in the park. One Sunday morning we were on deck having elevenses when a bevy of young girls walking by the ship stopped and looked up. A deck hand supposed to be a wee bit simple and nicknamed Tiko Spanish for cuckoo looked over and shouted something down to them. They shouted something in reply. He knew no Spanish but asked to borrow a jacket and wearing this, trousers and slippers he went down the gangway and stood with these girls for a few minutes then they all walked from the ship. He did not return until the following day.

The Seamans Mission was open every day and was run by an Irish catholic priest. There was a billiard table, dominoes, table tennis and in the evening there was dancing. There was even a beer bar and thinking this to be rather odd I asked why he sold beer. His answer was a good one. Here in the Mission the beer is cheaper and you are less likely to meet the troubles you may encounter in town. All the hostesses spoke English and one was Virginia her surname like most of the other girls was unpronounceable.

The priest arranged a football match between the MV African Prince and a local ameteur team. At half time we were losing by three goals to none. Ten minutes into the second half we scored a goal and a few minutes later scored another. After resuming play the referee unbelievingly blew his whistle for full time. The result was in the local sports papers next evening.

Mays Bar in Vinqt de Cinq de Mayo was run by an Irish lady and was very popular with merchant seamen. I saw very few locals in this bar.

One evening walking down Florida which is a very busy street a car came speeding down the road and was being chased by a police car its siren wailing and the police leaning out of the windows brandishing guns. People were diving into doorways, some were lying on the pavement. The cars passed me twice before driving along the riverside road. An account in the newspaper next day reported that the car had crashed several kilometers out of BA. and the occupants arrested. It also reported the coldest night in BA with the first frost in more than twenty years.

Jackie and me went to a circus and saw acrobats, clowns, lions, tigers, seals, sea lions. horses, elephants and parrots all doing their own routine. The clowns were exceptionally funny and I found them most entertaining. There was no need to understand Spanish. The noise from the children drowned the dialogue.

Every day boats loaded with lowing cattle could be seen and heard on the way up river to Rosario. On a return trip these same boats were laden with cattle but now as corned beef in tins.

We expected to return to New York which meant sailing through the tropics again and into Americas summer season.. With this in mind most of the crew had their heads shaved clean. Then came a change of orders which embarrassed them. We were to carry a cargo to London. Imagine being in your own home town in 1947 with your head shorn of hair. Our expected long tour was changed to just a few months. I sent a letter to my parents and one to Ruth telling them of the change and that the ships movements are posted in the library next door to the Town Hall in Fawcett St.

Two hours after leaving BA the main engine oil pump broke down resulting in the white metal running out of the thrust pads. To have them replaced we limped in to Montevideo on the opposite bank to BA and a few miles down the Rio de la Platt.

We tied up alongside the Tacoma which had been one of the supply ships to the pocket battleship Admiral Graf Von Spee. It had sought refuge here during the battle of the River Plate in December 1939 and was interned. Apparently it never left here. I clearly saw the name Tacoma on the stern. If the remains of the Graf Von Spee were still here I did not see them.

We were unable to go ashore and for the next three days we worked on the damaged propeller shaft before fitting the new pads. When these were fitted and tested OK we weighed anchor and set a course for London.

An albatross kept us company for a long time. It glided over us but never settled on the ship. Sometimes it would fly ought of sight for short periods then return. After crossing the equator we never saw it again.

For most of the six weeks voyage we never saw land but often saw several porpoises in a line leaping out of the ocean giving the allusion that we were looking at a sea serpent. For a few hours a whale kept us company. Once again I saw a shoal of flying fish probably being chased and trying to leap over our beam to escape. Some landed on the deck and were collected by the steward and for a few days supplemented our meals.

MY RETURN TO CIVVY STREET

London

During the crossing we were given a scare lasting almost two weeks. A radio message put us on war alert. Apparently there was trouble with Russia and we were warned to black out the ship at night as Russian submarines were in the vicinity and hostilities were possible. This was round about the start of the cold war with Russia. We experienced no incidents.

It was very early morning when we berthed in London and the Custom Officers came on board.

The so called simpleton approached the officers before they were ready to carry out their duties and he asked them if they could deal with him first so as to enable him to catch a train he knew would be leaving in an hour. Without examining his goods they gave him the all clear and off he went with a lot of stuff without having to pay duty.

The rest of us were thoroughly screened but very little duty was paid.

I arrived home late in the afternoon. Settling down with my parents I gave a brief account of my adventures

After allowing time for Ruth to get home from work and to have her tea I set off to visit her. I knocked on her door and it was answered by her sister. We did not know each other so she called for Ruth to come out. She came to the door holding a paint brush in her hand and wearing a paint smeared smock. When she saw me she said "Don`t go away" and disappeared. On her return a few second later without smock and brush we embraced and I knew then that we were bound together as were on our last meeting but this time our lives together would go on for another forty-five years.

After our embrace we went inside and I was introduced to members of her family. Her Mother, Sister Isabel, Brother Tom and Aunt Maggie who had come to live with them after Husband Jim Goffin was killed in a road accident a few years earlier.

For the first two weeks we walked a lot. On the cliff tops at Grangetown, Ryhope and at Whitburn. The South Hylton riverside. Penshaw Hill and Lovers Lane before it was swallowed up in the new Grindon Estate now being created. We also danced at Wetheralls.

At the end of my leave I was faced with having to decide my future. Do I return to my ship or do I remain on shore?.

Living with married or engaged shipmates I was able to see how they coped. I came to the conclusion that with the pact I had made with Ruth and how close our relationship was now and bringing to mind the behaviour of some of my past colleagues I thought it best for me to come ashore.

I still had a strong feeling to go back and with some regret, I sent in my resignation to the Prince Line Shipping Company and then visited the Shipping Office in Tatham St to resign from the Shipping Pool. I am no longer in the Merchant Navy and once again a landlubber. The decision was mine only. Ruth said she would accept whatever I decided to do. I believe that had I gone away she would have waited for my return.

1948

After leaving the MN I went back to Doxfords to work and went straight on to day and night shifts on alternative weeks. During my dinner break when on day shift

7-30am-6-00pm. I would meet Ruth near the watch strap factory where she worked.

We never met when I was night shift 6-00pm-7-30am

One dinner time leaving Doxfords to meet Ruth who did I see coming through the gate? None other than Marion Krzak from Baltimore USA.

She is now married and on holiday with her husband staying with his parents in General Havelock Rd. Having met several lads from Doxfords in the Merchant Navy Club in Baltimore during the war years she is hoping to meet some of them today.

On Saturdays we had tea at my Mams then went dancing at Wetheralls and on Sundays I had tea with Ruth and the other members of the family.

After tea her Uncle Jack and Aunt Alice usually called in. With them, Aunt Maggie and Brother Tom we played different card games, the most popular was Nap.

On Thursdays when Ruth finished work at 6-0pm she went straight over to Mams.

When I finished work I travelled by train to Monkwearmouth arriving at 7-00pm. A few minutes later I was home and my Mam served tea. An hour later Aunt Louise and Aunt Fran called and we all played Domino Whist.

When I was on dayshift we continued with our long walks. With the coming of the dark nights dancing to Jackie Browns band at Wetheralls on Saturdays with Ruths friend Mary Andrews now married to Jimmy Hunter and living in Murton. In mid-week the Bay Hotel at Seaburn dancing to Felix Mendholsen and his Hawaiin orchestra. Once a month a Social Evening was held in the Church of the Good Shepherd and we attended most of them and there I met Father Webber the Priest in charge and several friends of Ruth. On Easter Monday we went on a church outing to Beamish.

It is March and my sixth month on shore. My work was turning out engine parts of steel on a lathe and I hardly ever moved from it all shift and after working in the engine room, steering machinery, winches, windlass and other areas of a ship which needed my services I was finding it difficult to settle down. I asked for and was given a transfer to the quay where ships were fitted out with the main engine and auxiliary machinery.

Sometimes working in the engine rooms then a spell on the deck or the steering gear I was beginning to settle down. Unfortunately for me after a couple of weeks I was sent to work on the MV Interpreter being built on the stocks. This situation was just as bad as being on a lathe. I would work in one spot for one day and then do similar work at another spot. I felt cramped. I decided that I had had enough and I looked elsewhere for something more in my line.

I thought that I had found it when I moved to Readheads in High Shields I was given the job of making and installing the lubricating system for the steam engines under construction and then go out on the ships sea trials. The three vessels were SS Irish Oak, SS Fred Christiansun and SS Belevelyn.

Certain foods were still being rationed and in most heavy industries where manual work was being carried out extra coupons were given so as to buy more tea and sugar. These were supposed to increase and maintain energy enabling workers to do hard and heavy work. At Readheads I became friendly with Jimmy Grifiths a fitter who lived in Jarow. He was courting a South

Shields girl. Her name was Lena. Before they were married we often visited them at her home in South Shields.

Other workmates were Eric Old, Stan Davies and George Gray, I knew him from Doxfords early in the war,

We were now seriously considering marriage and began to look for a house and found a one in Hawthorn St. South in Millfield. It was mid-way between our two homes.

We did not borrow a mortgage. I thought that it would prove to be too expensive. Most of our money went into buying the house outright and a triplex oven to replace the existing fireplace.

Some time was spent cleaning the place out and laying linoleum. Wallpaper was scarce and very expensive so Sarah Ruths sister stippled the living room walls. Eric Old helped us with some of the smaller jobs.

When my brother Bob was in the army he was stationed in York and was billeted in the Bay Horse Hotel Monkbar run by Mr and Mrs Atha and when he learned that Ruth and Me were intending to go to York for a holiday in the summer he recommended that we go to that hotel. We took his advice

While there we visited the Cathedral, walked along the city walls and boating on the river. Ruth was in the WAAFs for a lot of the war and one of her postings was in the nearby Linton Airfield and we went there one day. We liked our time here so much we stayed an extra week-end and travelled back on Monday.

During the festive season we were invited to parties at the respective homes of all of our relatives and close friends

1949

WEDDING OF RUTH AND GEORGE

Wedding of Ruth and George the author 1949

We decided to have a quiet wedding and so arranged for the ceremony to take place on Wednesday the 16th February. This brought a howl of protest from both our families complaining that most would be at work. Under immense pressure we submitted and the date was changed to Saturday19th February.

All relatives and close friends were invited to the wedding in The Church of the Good Shepherd and the reception in Franklin St Hall Millfield. Work friends of Ruth and mine from Readheads were invited to the reception.

When the 16th February dawned there was a covering of snow 2" deep. On the morning of the 19th the sun was shining and all of the snow had gone. It was a lovely Spring day. I called at my barber shop to have my hair trimmed then went home to await the taxi to take me to the church. When it arrived the driver said that he remembered bringing me home from the station about four years back with a lot of luggage. Approaching the church he suggested that there was still time to change my mind and go back home.

Entering the Church marked the end of my Single Days

1 October 2009

My Single Days 1921 to 1949

APPENDICES
APPENDIX I

COLLIERY AND SEA RD FIRST AID POSTS. FAP 1940-1943

Many of the volunteers
Gerry Anderson. Pamela Anderson. Albert Beatty. George Bell the author. Gordon Bell. Jim Bewick. George Buckley. John Buckley. Jack Cartwright.

Mickey Conlin. Howard Crooks. Hilda Crooks. Willa Crooks. Edith Crozier. Jack Crozier. Billy Davison. Doris Day. Jean Dennett. Nancy Dodds. Hendie Ellison. George Farquar. Stan Franklin. Mr Charles Gardner. Mrs Edith Gardner. Edith Gardner. Rita Gardner. Kitty Gibson. Tom Graham. Nancy Graham. Mr Roy Hird. Mrs Elsie Hird. Gerry Holland. Lance Kirkhouse. Mary Kirton. Ena Kirton. Walter Knox. Violet Knox. Jack Lillie. George Lumsdon. Mr Alf Madden. Mrs Margaret Madden. Doris Marshall Mr Charlie McBain. Ruth McBain. Vera McBain. John Punshen. Jack Snowdon. Norman Snowdon. Bobby Stokoe. Mary Teasdale. Tommy Watson. Aurial Welch. Donald Cooper. Jack Crozier. Edith Crozier. Billy Davison. Billy Stokoe Alf Graham.

My Single Days 1921 to 1949

MY APOLOGIES FOR NAMES MISSPELLED OR OMITTED

APPENDICES
APPENDIX II

SOME OF THE CREW ON THE MV EMPIRE HOUSMAN

Mr Gilbert Chief engineer Cardiff
2nd " Newcastle
3rd " Costa Rica
Joe Lawson 4th " Pallion
George Bell 5th " Monkwearmouth
Bill Francis 6th " Southwick
Mr Lewis Captain Cardiff
Mr Bamborough 2nd Mate Durham
Mr Wynn 3rd Mate Newcastle
Neil Bell Apprentice Loch Boisdale South Uist
Bob Sugarman Steward Belgium
Ron Taylor Steward ?

My Single Days 1921 to 1949

APPENDICES
APPENDIX III

SOME OF THE CREW ON MV HOPECREST 1944

Mr Egglestone Captain South Shields
Apprentice Bernard Ford South Shields
Bill Reed Chief engineer South Shields
Mr Waters 2nd " Whitley Bay
George Cross 3rd " Newcastle
Joe Lawson 4th " Sunderland
George Bell Junior " Sunderland
Billy Robinson Junior " Sunderland
Sid Larson Junior " Longbenton
Ted Kennedy Junior " Newcastle
Mr Chisholm Donkeyman Workington

My Single Days 1921 to 1949

MY APOLOGIES FOR NAMES MISSPELLED OR OMITTED

APPENDICES
APPENDIX IV

SOME OF THE CREW ON THE MV WELSH PRINCE

Mr Proctor Captain Willington Quay
Norman Gail 1st Mate London
Michael Boggs 2nd " Australia
Andy Bell 3rd " Edinburgh
John Kerslake 1st Apprentice Swansea
Steve Beighton 2nd " Huddersfield
Mr Payne 3rd " Cornwall
Mr Bradford Chief Steward Glasgow
Harry Clarkson Chief engineer Whitby
Albert Redford 2nd " Silksworth
Arthur Harrison 3rd " Wallsend
Norman Buckley 4th " North Shields
George Bell 5th " Sunderland
Hans Bulmer 6th " Heaton
Mr Vickerman Chippy Hull
Sid Dorman Chief Sparks London
Jack Aitchison 2nd " Edinburgh
John Ellis 3rd " Edinburgh

My Single Days 1921 to 1949

APPENDICES
APPENDIX V

SOME OF THE CREW ON THE MV AFRICAN PRINCE

Mr Martin Captain ?
Mr Cook Chief engineer
George Bell 4th " Sunderland
Jackie Atkinson 5th " Philadelphia near Sunderland
John Mars 6th " Glasgow

My Single Days 1921 to 1949

MY APOLOGIES FOR NAMES MISSPELLED OR OMITTED

APPENDICES
APPENDIX VI

THE CHURCH OF THE GOOD SHEPHERD 1948

Father Webber, Priest in charge

Some of the congregation
Ivy Coulthard. John Bull and his sister Elsie. Mrs Conlee. Mr and Mrs Fairbairn. Peggy Fairbairn. Charlie Goodrich. Bella Gordon. Ruth Gordon. John Henshall. Hilda Kylo. Mrs Richardson. Iris Thompson. John Wilson. Mr and Mrs Whitfield. 1